Value Creation through Executive Development

The ability of organisations to generate long-term value and growth depends to a very large extent on the capacity of the executive cohort to conceive and implement strategic initiatives through a well-motivated and enabled workforce. However, generating consistent value in today's volatile, uncertain, complex and ambiguous (VUCA) and rapidly evolving digital economic landscape can be challenging and, therefore, executives need to update their capabilities regularly to align with the changing value drivers required for long-term growth. To achieve the expected value and growth at a more sustainable level, executive development must be managed as a strategic asset and optimised through effective design and implementation and the effects must be proactively evaluated through meaningful leading indicators and actual 'hard' measures.

Value Creation through Executive Development, therefore, offers a well-supported and clearly structured approach to address the gap between executive development initiatives and the creation of long-term organisational value and growth. This book provides a valuable resource to executives and management development professionals who have experienced frustration about the lack of non-value-adding executive development programmes. It also serves as a professional resource for managers of executive and management development programmes, organisational development departments and organisational development consultants, allowing them to integrate this material into existing programmes to achieve value-centric outcomes and to achieve long-term performance targets. Additionally, it serves as a teaching resource for participants in executive/management development courses or seminars globally; offering them the capacity to implement value-centric initiatives and gain the capacity to influence the tactical, operational and strategic dimensions of their organisational performance.

Solomon Akrofi is the Director and founder of Leapmax Consulting, a management consultancy, focusing on designing and embedding executive leadership capabilities to drive organisational success.

Value Creation through Executive Development

Solomon Akrofi

Routledge
Taylor & Francis Group

LONDON AND NEW YORK

First published 2019
by Routledge
2 Park Square, Milton Park, Abingdon, Oxon OX14 4RN

and by Routledge
711 Third Avenue, New York, NY 10017

Routledge is an imprint of the Taylor & Francis Group, an informa business

British Library Cataloguing-in-Publication Data
A catalogue record for this book is available from the British Library

Library of Congress Cataloging-in-Publication Data
Names: Akrofi, Solomon, 1971- author.
Title: Value creation through executive development / Solomon Akrofi.
Description: Abingdon, Oxon; New York, NY: Routledge, 2019.
Identifiers: LCCN 2018030864 | ISBN 9781138575578 (hardback) | ISBN 9781351271561 (ebook) | ISBN 9781351271547 (epub3) | ISBN 9781351271530 (mobipocket)
Subjects: LCSH: Executives. | Performance. | Value. | Corporations—Valuation. | Management.
Classification: LCC HD38.2 .A54 2019 | DDC 658.4/07124—dc23
LC record available at https://lccn.loc.gov/2018030864

ISBN: 978-1-138-57557-8 (hbk)
ISBN: 978-1-351-27156-1 (ebk)

Typeset in Bembo
by codeMantra

This book is dedicated to my wife Rita, to my children Meridith, David, Samuel and Michael, and also to my parents, James and Grace.

Contents

Figures

Tables

Acknowledgements

I am greatly indebted to many people who have contribute to my life journey, beginning with both of my parents who provided the support and love to strive for excellence, to many friends and other individuals who supported me during challenging moments of my life.

To my wife Rita, I am most grateful to you for providing me with the drive and impetus to remain focused in completing this book. From the depth of my heart, I thank my beloved children, Meridith, David, Samuel and Michael for their love and patience for the precious time they lost whilst I completed this work.

Many thanks to Kristina Abbotts at Routledge for believing in this project as without her, this book may not have seen the light of day. To the editorial and production team at Routledge; Christiana Mandizha, Daniel Fowler and all those involved in the cover design and other stages of production, I am grateful for your excellent support. I am also thankful to Katy Hamilton for the excellent development edit work and to Nicola Prior for providing copy editing of the final manuscript.

I deeply value the contributions of Simon Burtonshaw-Gunn (Professor of Industrial Management and Head of Division at Northampton Business School), John Burgoyne (Professor of Leadership at Lancaster University), Christiane Feenstra (Founder and Owner of Executive Dialogues and Formal Global Head of Strategic Resourcing & Talent – Swiss Re, Switzerland) and John Dutton (Director at Steer Group) for reading the manuscript and offering constructive comments, which helped to shape the final content of this book.

Lastly, I thank you immensely for taking time to explore the content of this book and I hope it will transform your approach to developing executive talent for your organisation.

Introduction

Executives have a compelling and strategic responsibility for creating and protecting long-term organisational value which they achieve by responding rapidly to changing business contexts, diffusing the disruptive threats posed by start-ups and competitors and building a solid talent base capable of continually driving a pipeline of distinctive innovative services and products which can enhance customer experience and long-term growth. In order to achieve and maintain a virtuous cycle of value creation and to fend off existential threats, organisations invest heavily in various development interventions thinking that it is a silver bullet. However, most executive development programmes tend to be generic and fail to provide the much-needed focus of generating long-term value creation and growth. This lack of emphasis on value-creation has not limited the level of investment in executive development. This continuous investment is partly in response to the intense talent wars to retain and attract employees capable of creating disruptive business models and also the perception that developing the executive and leadership cohort within an organisation will automatically generate value, regardless of alignment with organisational value drivers. According to Bersin by Deloitte,[1] the estimated investment in leadership in the United States alone, in 2013, was approximately US$15.5 billion and this is bound to increase exponentially as the talent wars intensify into the digital economy. Unfortunately, the colossal investment in executive development is not generating the expected value. A joint study by University of North Carolina Kenan-Flagler Business School and the Human Capital Institute (HCI) in 2014[2] found that, although 85 per cent of respondents agree that there is an urgent need to accelerate the development of their executives and leaders, only 40 per cent report that their high potential employees can meet future business needs.

Hence, there is a compelling opportunity for a book which offers a structured approach to closing the gap between executive development initiatives, business needs and long-term organisational value creation and growth.

The ability of organisations to generate long-term value and growth depends to a large extent on the capacity of the executive cohort to conceive and implement strategic initiatives through a well-motivated and enabled workforce. Generating consistent value in today's volatile, uncertain, complex and ambiguous (VUCA) where organisations are grappling with the impact of globalisation, digitisation and rapidly changing customer expectations can be a challenging feat and therefore executives need to update their capabilities regularly to align with the changing value drivers required for long-term growth. To achieve the expected value and growth at a more sustainable and consistent level, executive development must be managed as a strategic asset and optimised through effective design and implementation, and the effects must be proactively evaluated and adjusted to align with the strategic direction and objectives of the organisation.

In order to close the gap between executive development interventions and organisational performance, consideration should be given to the entire end to end process from design to measurement to ensure that it aligns with organisational value drivers. The design of executive development interventions must account for the unique characteristics of executives to enhance retention of knowledge and application, as well as, consideration of the pros and cons of different development modalities so that the most relevant ones can be selected and this process must also account for interventions better suited to different levels of executives to ensure that the anticipated return on investment can be maximised. In addition, executive development interventions must be designed to address current challenges with provisions made for future organisational challenges and trends, including the emerging digital economy, artificial intelligence, machine learning, robotics and automation so that the organisation can be well prepared to instigate disruptive business models ahead of competitors. Also, the approach to executive development must cover the organisational perspective as well as the management of participants within a wider ecosystem as this is increasingly becoming a viable model for creating sustainable value, disruptive models and for expanding into new business models and markets. A one-size-fits-all/off-the-shelf and generic approach to executive development should be avoided by ensuring that the development interventions, including the learning needs analysis process is tailored to specific organisational needs, culture, and sector challenges, with adequate levels of personalisation for individual executives to maximise the likely return on investment from such interventions.

Executives must also have the capacity to realign their organisational architecture at the strategic, tactical and operational levels to translate the outputs/outcomes of executive development interventions to drive value creation. This requires creating a collective leadership mindset and dismantling authoritarian cultures, and entrenching cross-departmental collaboration to embed an enabling environment ripe for creating disruptions and innovations to enhance customer experience which will ultimately result in value creation and long-term growth.

Adequate preparation for ROI evaluations by making early provision for this during the development need analysis stage ensures that data requirements, frequency and formats are agreed well in advance of the executive development interventions. This will smoothen the post-development measurement process and minimise the lack of motivation to track the outcomes of development interventions and computation of the ROI.

All of these concepts are covered within this book with relevant examples, case studies and concepts from global organisations such as IBM, Cisco, BP, and Microsoft, with digestible takeaways, models and ideas for readers to drive a value-centred approach to developing executive development for long-term survival. A brief summary of the contents of each chapter is outlined as follows:

Chapter 1 establishes the connection between executive development and the value creation processes of organisations. This is achieved by highlighting the core drivers required for generating value from both organic growth and business combination growth, whilst connecting these growth drivers to executive development interventions.

Chapter 2 maps out the capabilities executives need to acquire in order to achieve and embed value-centricity in a consistent manner. These capabilities are aligned with the organic and business combinations drivers identified in the previous chapter to provide connection with the organisational value-creation processes.

Chapter 3 outlines different approaches that organisations can deploy to build value-centric executive development architecture and considers formal and informal learning, social and learning technology. These approaches take into account crucial factors in maximising the benefits of executive development interventions, such as stage of organisational growth, firm size and sector dynamics.

Chapter 4 addresses the importance of making executive development programmes work for organisations specific needs and avoiding the 'magic bullet' and 'one-size-fits-all' approaches, which can be counterproductive and ineffective in driving the desired organisational impact and outcomes on business drivers. It recaps some of the content already looked at in other chapters but the focus is reflective and addresses how executive development interventions can be designed to align with the unique characteristics of the organisation, rather than offering a universal solution. Specific factors that are addressed include organisational size considerations, learning needs assessment process for executives, how executive development can be tailored to address cultural climate challenges, sector dynamics and how appropriate digital technology and platforms can be effectively integrated into the learning architecture.

Chapter 5 details how the alignment between executive development and organisational strategy can be achieved in a structured manner, to ensure synergy between the two critical organisational processes to drive value. This is achieved via an eight-step method which aligns strategic value drivers with executive development to ensure that learning is embedded in the organisation and therefore growth is sustainable.

Chapter 6 provides a structured approach to enable organisations to bridge the gap between executive development initiatives and organisational performance. This delves into steps that executives and organisations can embark on to realign their organisational architecture at the strategic, tactical and operational levels to translate the outputs/outcomes of executive development initiatives to drive value-centricity and long-term growth.

Chapter 7 offers an incremental approach to measuring the impact of executive development initiatives based on business value impact and other parameters. Evaluating ROI is often perceived to be too challenging due to the intangible nature of executive learning but this chapter will show what to measure and how to identify deviation from targets to enable corrective action to be taken, thereby maximising return on investment on executive development initiatives.

This book is written to serve three distinct but related audiences. First, it will provide a valuable resource to executives and management development professionals who have experienced frustration about the lack of non-value-adding executive development programmes and who—because they are passionate about transforming their organisations—are searching for innovative ideas and concepts which they can tap into to transform the approach to executive development in their organisations to drive long-term value.

Secondly, the book will serve as a professional resource for managers of executive and management development programmes, organisational development departments and organisational development consultants, allowing them to integrate this material into existing programmes in order to achieve value-centric outcomes and to achieve long-term performance targets.

Thirdly, the book will serve as a teaching resource for participants in executive/management development courses or seminars globally; offering them the capacity to implement value-centric initiatives successfully and gain the capacity to influence the tactical, operational and strategic dimensions of their organisational performance.

Readers of this book will:

- Gain the capacity to improve long-term organisational viability and success through systematic executive development that focuses on value-creation.
- Become adept at designing value-centric executive development interventions from scratch and link them to the strategic and critical organisational value drivers.
- Have the capacity to link various strategic initiatives to the executive development initiatives to maximise the impact of development interventions on organisational outcome.
- Shape organisational architecture (culture, value & systems) to create an enabling environment where employee potential can be optimised to drive organisational outcomes at the strategic, operational and tactical levels.

- Increase the accountability for performance and development of executives and senior managers to drive long-term organisational value.
- Significantly enhance the cost-benefit ratio for executive development programmes.
- Arrange existing executive development programmes in a systematic sequence, so that participants can use the information in earlier modules to reinforce and embed information in subsequent modules.
- Derive the capacity to effectively contribute to executive and management development programmes which will result in improved skills, attitudes, behaviour and performance.

The book will:

Provide specific examples of how leading companies in Europe, Asia and US have successfully designed and implemented value-centric executive development.

Outline simple and practical techniques and models for designing, implementing and embedding value-centric executive development within organisations

Provide a unique and incremental method to monitor and measure the effects of executive development interventions on organisational outcomes and examples of how other companies have mapped and embedded a value-centric executive development measurement model.

Notes

1. Patti Phillips, 'Measuring the Success of Leadership Development' (Association for Talent Development, 22 July 2015) https://www.td.org/insights/measuring-the-success-of-leadership-development (last accessed 30 July 2017).
2. Human Capital Institute, 'How to Accelerate Leadership Development' (University of North Carolina Kenan-Flagler Business School and the Human Capital Institute 2015) https://www.kenan-flagler.unc.edu/~/media/Files/documents/executive-development/unc-leadership-survey-2014-accelerating-leadership-development.pdf?la=en&la=en(last accessed 30 July 2017).

Executive development and value creation for business growth

Executives at all levels and stages of their careers need to recognise that developing, and the rapid application of new capabilities is a new currency for driving organisational growth and survival. Developing the right set of capabilities also provides the capacity for executives to adapt quickly in uncertain times and lay the foundation for long-term organisational growth. Hence, there is a greater imperative for executives to become used to learning and unlearning at a rapid rate. At the same time, organisations need to recognise and manage executive development as a core strategic driver of value and growth and not just implement it as a tick-box exercise where executives engage in a plethora of programmes with no direct link to organisational growth and survival.

The cases of Nokia and Kodak exemplify why executive development is crucial for organisational survival. Having pioneered and launched the world's first mass-produced mobile phone (Nokia 1011) in 1992, Nokia held a dominant share of the global mobile market throughout the 1990s until it relinquished this enviable position to Samsung and Apple, both of which have a much wider portfolio of businesses to cushion them from the shocks of the mobile phone industry. Nokia's management team did not only fail to respond to emerging disruptors such as Apple and Samsung, and the shifting consumer experience from the Symbian platform (on which Nokia phones were developed) to App-based platforms such as the iOS and Android, but they also failed to anticipate competition in the lower end of the market, from manufacturers such as HTC, Huawei and ZTE, who reduced the market share of Nokia in emerging markets by offering cost-effective handsets with more powerful functionalities and features compared to Nokia's offerings.[1]

Nokia's top management also lost the technologically and the strategically integrative decision capabilities required to set priorities and to reposition itself against the pressure of disruptive competitors and the low-cost manufactures which eventually resulted in the eventual shrinking of the business to a network infrastructure provider.[2]

Nokia's rapid decline exemplifies an organisation in which executives failed to leverage and translate a unique selling proposition into long-term sustainable financial growth. Kodak is another classic example of an organisation which fell from prominence to extinction owing to strategy deficiency of executives in converting vast intellectual capital into value-generating products.

Although Kodak built on its strengths in organic chemistry and optics to create some profitable products, however, the organisation failed when it tried to launch new business models and products based on existing capabilities and hence significantly undermined its ability to benefit from the digitisation of the photo and motion picture industry.[3]

These two firms, and indeed several other organisations, have been driven from a dominant market share position to complete oblivion in this era of volatility, uncertainty, constant change and ambiguity (VUCA), where business models across industries are becoming obsolete rapidly.

The commodities sector (oil, gas and metals), for example, experienced a sharp decline between 2014 and 2016. This resulted from the over-expansive production (owing to low borrowing cost) without predicting the weakening demand (for natural resources like steel, iron ore and crude oil) from China and other emerging economies.[4]

The most efficient operators such as Rio Tinto and BHP Billiton have profited from economies of scale and the lower cost capabilities they have developed over the decades, whilst others such as platinum miner Lonmin – with a previous market capitalisation of £6 billion – failed to survive the turbulence and have been taken over by South African peer Sibanye-Stillwater valuing the company at £285 million.[5]

Businesses in the commodities sector are adapting their business models to align with lower profit margins or otherwise face extinction owing to the dependency of this sector on uncertain and unpredictable demand factors from emerging economies. For example, Anglo American is focusing its operations on three products – Diamond, Platinum and Copper and has veered away from iron ore, coal, nickel, phosphate and manganese, as these were less profitable compared to the three retained products. The retail sector is also undergoing rapid transformation with the onslaught of digitisation and technology, which will shrink the workforce used in traditional brick-and-motor models. Uber and Airbnb have also disrupted existing industrial business models by utilising technology and digitisation by taking advantage of the platform business model to meet customer needs across a wider geographic audience at the fraction of the cost incurred by traditional business models in the urban transportation and hospitality sectors. The effects of the VUCA environment on businesses are exacerbated further by ever-shifting customer expectations for greater customisation coupled with uncontrollable events such as natural disasters, epidemics and geo-political tensions, which make prediction of future profitability almost impossible. These external factors influence the capacity for organisations to create consistent value and financial growth.

Value and growth defined

Organisational value is created at the micro and macro level. At the micro level, value creation is driven by an organisation's capacity to produce unique products or services for customers better than competitors. The value creation capability can be expanded further at the macro level by enhancing the business model, acquiring other businesses or combining these approaches. If value creation activities are managed effectively, the consequence should be measurable long-term sustainable organisational growth, which is the growth rate an organisation can achieve without increasing its financial leverage or debt financing levels. In other words, this reflects the growth rate generated by the organisation from the reinvestment of normal earnings and through the prudent management of financial resources.

However, the generic drivers of growth tend to differ across sectors (e.g. occupancy rates in the hotel sector, sales per square feet in the retailers sector and patent conversion rates for pharmaceutical firms) and influence the strategic decisions that executives have to make across their portfolio of businesses.[6] The sustainable growth rate is also influenced by three key variables: profit margin, capital investment intensity, expected growth rate versus cost of capital, and the combined effect of all three variables on the business models and revenue streams available to the organisation.[7]

Most often organisations grapple with the internal effects of inertia as they approach the pinnacle of the growth cycle. Some industries, like the insurance sector, are becoming more vulnerable as they approach the point of saturation with diminished margins and very little product differentiation, as the pressures of digitisation intensify with automation likely to replace various specialisms in the underwriting specialist in the insurance sector. As organisations traverse the growth cycle, they face a self-imposed threat posed by the propensity to lapse into a natural inertia, and they become less responsive to external threats and opportunities. This inertia, if not cured swiftly, can eventually normalise reactive behaviours and less adaptive cultures, such as in the case of Nokia in the mobile phone sector which starved their innovative pipeline and diminished the aggressive mentality required to drive survival and growth of the organisation.

All of these internal and external threats to organisational growth and survival provide a compelling case for executives to embrace an agile and continuous learning mentality with the acquisition of new capabilities being the norm. These are some of the main reasons why executive development is relevant at all levels of the organisational hierarchy, and must be supported by the right diagnostics of capability gaps, design, implementation and measurement to deliver the intended organisational outcome. All of these will be discussed in much greater depth in Chapters 3 and 4.

Who is an executive?

Executives include the chief executive officer (CEO), and the C-suite (chief marketing officer, chief information officer, chief technology officer, chief finance officer, chief innovation officer), senior vice presidents, divisional directors and their direct reports (two-three tiers below the C-suite) who are responsible for formulating long-range strategic plans (five years), conducting high-level boundary management activities and providing inspiration and talent management across the entire organisation.

According to a Harvard Business Review Research, the size of the executive team in large businesses has increased, rising from about five in the mid-1980s to almost ten in the mid-2000s'.[8] This trend in the growth of the executive team size seems to be unabating with new titles such as Chief Robotic Officer, Chief Growth Officer and Chief Digital Officer emerging as organisations position themselves to address some of the complex challenges posed by disruptive competitors and decline in growth opportunities across industries.

Executives exemplify leadership behaviour in setting organisation-wide objectives, engaging in external communications and promotions to stakeholders and clients and coordinating activities across multiple departments. In addition, they carry the ultimate responsibility for delivering the overarching organisational-level performance targets, and focus on exceeding client expectations. Widening the scope of executives to include leaders two − three tiers below the C-suite depending on organisational structure and size is premised on the fact that these lower-level executives not only provide crucial input in the formulation of strategy, they also have much closer proximity and interaction with customers and the ecosystem and have better visibility of organisational resources required for driving organisational value.

For example, the head of product innovation will provide crucial input in the formulation of a business model or even be involved in due diligence activities for an acquisition which will drive long-term value creation. The contribution of lower-tier executives to the decision-making process challenges any possible group-think effects and biases at the top of the organisation and enables the integration of customer and employee perspectives to the strategy formulation and implementation process. Therefore, these individuals should be embraced into the 'executive' fold and provided with the necessary development and experience required to contribute effectively towards value creation as well as strengthen the executive bench. Finally, research indicates that business unit leaders outside the C-suite are accountable for up to 29 per cent of disruptive growth (which is growth emanating from the creation of new markets and differentiated products and services which will eventually

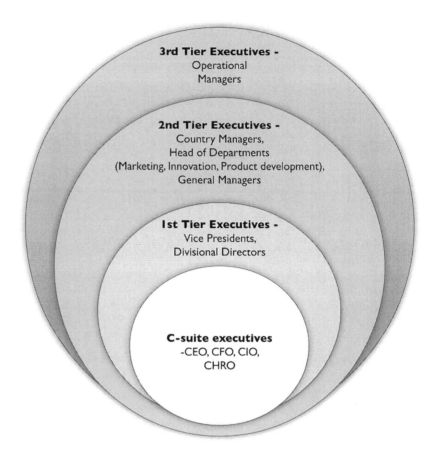

Figure 1.1 The executive level onion – layers of organisational executives.

displace existing offerings from competitors) which offers a compelling case for development interventions to be expanded outside the traditional executive ring.[9] These lower tier executives – who have better understanding of the operational challenges, customer preferences and can combine data with strategic insight to deliver superior customer experience – need to be offered compelling development opportunities to create disruptive growth.

What is development?

Development at the executive level is considered to encapsulate the systematic improvement and broadening of knowledge, experience and capabilities of personal qualities and attributes required for the successful execution of organisational challenges in current and future context.[10] Such development also involves the process of embracing increasing complexity as an organisation, and becoming more elaborate and differentiated, by virtue of learning and maturation, thereby opening up the potential for new ways of acting and responding to changes in the business environment.[11] In essence, development interventions must not only result in transformed behaviours, experiences and capabilities must be acted upon to drive value and improvements in organisational outputs. With executives, the acquisition and action dimensions of development can occur concurrently or even overlap, as a greater level of executive development tends to be informally oriented and embedded within the workplace. Both informal and formal development modalities will be looked into in much more detail in Chapter 3.

By maintaining a continuous development mindset, executives can avoid reliance on past accomplishments, experience and successes and keep looking for new frontiers of growth and value generation. Effective development will also prepare executives to be better prepared for challenges in the business environment, make informed choices, and move away from their comfort zone where growth is stagnated. Executives who also embrace continuous learning are able to shed non-productive behaviours and embrace new ones, which can be useful in driving the cultural and organisational change necessary for driving long-term growth.

What is executive development?

Development at the executive level must enhance both management and leadership capabilities and not only focus on the latter as the management capabilities required to drive value at the strategic level tend to focus on recognising, monitoring, interpreting and distributing information and resources across the organisation to drive effective execution of strategy rather than the coordination activities which occur at the operational level. Executives also deploy leadership capabilities to set compelling visions, craft enduring strategies, communicate across divisions and with different stakeholders, motivate and engage with employees from diverse cultures to deliver organisational objectives. Thus, executives need to combine these two facets effectively (leadership and management function) in order to drive organisational value, although leadership tends to be the more prominent focus at the higher levels of the executive hierarchy.

In essence, 'executive development encompasses the formal and informal learning interventions designed to drive improvement in learning behaviours, dynamic capabilities and human and social capital, which enables actors to offer better support and resources to employees, resulting in greater efficiencies, creativity, innovation and superior organisational performance'.[12]

The case for executive development is more compelling as executives' failure rate (attrition rate and inability to deliver strategic objectives they were engaged to deliver) according to a study by Harvard Business Review over a 10-year period is as high as 56 to 75 per cent, depending on the executive's position.[13]

Engaging in effective development initiatives will potentially not only reduce the high failure rates but also equip executives to create an enabling environment within their organisations that supports value creation and growth and empower executives to embed an agile organisational culture and business models which is responsive to short, medium and long-term needs of customers, stakeholders, society and the environment. Executives can assess if they are successful in creating and sustaining an enabling environment when their decisions, thinking, and actions resonate across all levels of the organisation and when employees reciprocate by offering new ideas, which can be rapidly tested, developed, and converted into new products and services.

Resistance from employees to new initiatives has been cited to be one of the top factors for the failure of strategy implementation.[14] This consolidates the need for executives to continuously develop the right capabilities in order to create an enabling environment for employees to contribute towards organisational objectives. For matured and older organisations this imperative is even greater as there is a potential to lose the agility and sense of urgency that start-ups and disrupters may embody.

Executive development must improve the functional deficiencies of individual executives and enable them to exert their full potential for the benefit of the organisation. Individual executive needs will differ from others within the cohort or team owing to functional differences, variations in the depth of experience, differential educational levels, and other unique biases and other idiosyncratic tendencies. Hence executive development must stimulate the capabilities of the entire executive cohort, as they learn through action learning methods (interactive in nature, provoke reflection and action), sharing of experiences and engage in group interactions (these will be covered in more depth in Chapter 3). Cisco, for example, considers the strength of its executive team from a portfolio perspective. For example, if the executive portfolio is composed mostly of strategic thinkers with no operational capability, then the organisation might suffer on the strategy execution side. If assessments unearth gaps in specific business capabilities – either technical or strategic – then appropriate development interventions will be implemented to bridge the gap.[15] We will look at how gaps in the individual and team capabilities can be identified in Chapter 4.

In the era of constant disruptions, executives have to constantly develop the right capabilities to enable them to respond to the challenges of reinventing business models and organisational culture to take advantage of new opportunities in the evolving digital economy and to ensure long-term organisational survival.

Connecting executive development to value creation (business growth)

Organisations create value and growth on several fronts, but these can be crystallised under two broad categories: organic growth and/or business combination and partnerships initiatives (see figure 1.2). The successful implementation of these initiatives requires executives to exhibit certain unique capabilities at the individual and collective levels. These unique capabilities must be harnessed consistently to create an enabling environment for employees to innovate and improve productivity levels and to enable executives to determine where future sources of value will emerge from and develop necessary strategic actions to capture it. Concurrently, executives

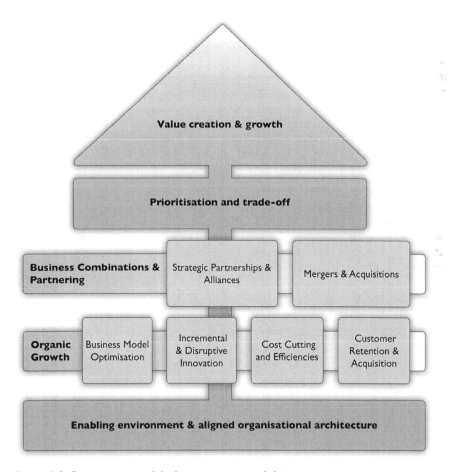

Figure 1.2 Business growth/value-creation model.

need to deploy these capabilities to align the overall organisational architecture (a nexus of processes, technology, culture and values) to drive customer-centric innovation in the short-term and at the same time prepare for emerging trends (including mega events) that can disrupt existing business models.

Creating the right environment for employees to maximise value to the organisation requires executives to deploy the right set of capabilities to identify the right talents and provide them support, exposure and assignments which enhance the production of innovative goods and services to generate value and sustainable growth. The role of executives as creators of 'enabling environments' for value creation, innovation and growth contrasted with the traditional view of being the paragons of organisational strategy will become more prevalent as organisations move into the digital economy, which is characterised by ecosystem models, sustained by disruptive innovations and driven by customer-centricity. Executives will still need to strategise but also need to cultivate enhanced capabilities to stimulate employees across different cultures and geographic locations to deliver consistent growth in intensely competitive landscapes.

However, owing to stagnation in traditional markets and challenges of transitioning successfully into emerging markets, delivering consistent growth can be a huge challenge, especially for large conglomerates and organisations such as Best Buy, Coca Cola, DigitasLBi, Mondelēz, Tyson Foods, Kellogg, PayPal, Colgate-Palmolive, and Coty who have bolstered their executive teams with Chief Growth Officers (CGO) to bring a strategic focus, acceleration and innovative approaches to expand into existing and potential market segments.

Intrinsic to the duty of care to shareholders, executives need to maintain strategic oversight over organisational resources and prioritise various strategic initiatives to deliver consistent value and growth and return on investments. This responsibility requires rebalancing and trading off the various initiatives to align with external and internal factors. Executives will need to possess the right capabilities to fulfil this crucial role effectively. This needs to be complemented by the team aspect of capability building, as a high performing executive team might complement each other by building on the strength of team capabilities. Maintaining strategic oversight and prioritising strategic initiatives require decision-making skills, which need to be honed consistently across the executive bench/and to match evolving business environments. Further details of the individual capabilities executives need to deliver value and growth will be discussed in more depth in Chapter 2.

The role of executive development in creating value is embedded within the entire fabric of an organisation. Figure 1.3 expands the two broad and complementary avenues through which organisations create value and growth: organic growth and/or business combination and partnerships.

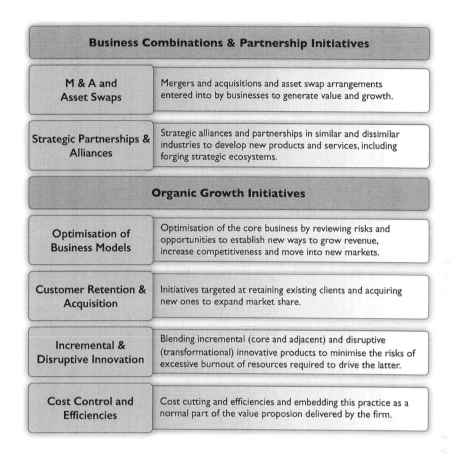

Business Combinations & Partnership Initiatives

M & A and Asset Swaps	Mergers and acquisitions and asset swap arrangements entered into by businesses to generate value and growth.
Strategic Partnerships & Alliances	Strategic alliances and partnerships in similar and dissimilar industries to develop new products and services, including forging strategic ecosystems.

Organic Growth Initiatives

Optimisation of Business Models	Optimisation of the core business by reviewing risks and opportunities to establish new ways to grow revenue, increase competitiveness and move into new markets.
Customer Retention & Acquisition	Initiatives targeted at retaining existing clients and acquiring new ones to expand market share.
Incremental & Disruptive Innovation	Blending incremental (core and adjacent) and disruptive (transformational) innovative products to minimise the risks of excessive burnout of resources required to drive the latter.
Cost Control and Efficiencies	Cost cutting and efficiencies and embedding this practice as a normal part of the value proposition delivered by the firm.

Figure 1.3 Organic growth and/or business combination and partnership initiatives.

Optimisation of business models: The optimisation of a firm's unique value proposition (UVP), revenue and operating models to drive expansion of product/service offering into new and existing markets is crucial for organic growth. In developing an optimum business model, executives must evaluate the risks and opportunities internal/external to the business environment to establish new ways of adding value, growing revenues and improving competitiveness. As competitiveness intensifies across several industries, executives need to combine a range of capabilities such as decision-making, forecasting, brand awareness and customer engagement and strong analytics skills to respond to mega events which can threaten the viability of existing business models.

Business model optimisation calls for executives to continuously review value propositions, operating and revenue models, pursue cost reduction and

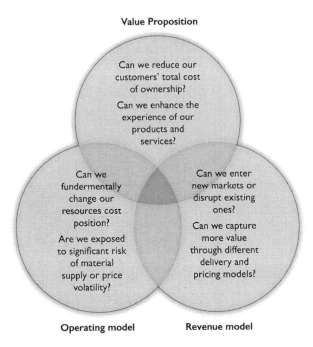

Value Proposition

Can we reduce our customers' total cost of ownership?

Can we enhance the experience of our products and services?

Can we fundermentally change our resources cost position?

Are we exposed to significant risk of material supply or price volatility?

Can we enter new markets or disrupt existing ones?

Can we capture more value through different delivery and pricing models?

Operating model   **Revenue model**

Figure 1.4 Business model optimisation.

growth opportunities, and examine different pricing models and opportunities to drive collaboration with the supply chain to deliver sustainable value to customers. This calls for executives to continuously expand their capabilities to match the external and internal factors impinging on the viability of firms' business models. Organisations can approach business model innovation within the digital era by taking an evolving approach or by launching disruptive business models depending on organisational resources, level of innovation culture and alertness to customer needs. The following section summarises some of the possible options available for launching evolving and disruptive digital business model innovation and a consideration of some of the capabilities that will be required at the executive level to execute them successfully.

Evolving digital business models

Selective Disruption Model: Involves investing in opportunities to neutralise disruptive threat, including disruptive technologies, specialist human capabilities and talent, innovative digitised processes, and acquiring companies with these attributes (e.g. Intel investing in Chargify,

Google's acquisition of Youtube). Some of the capabilities that executives will need to deliver this business model effectively include, faster identification of the intrinsic value of strategic target start-ups, trend-spotting (to determine where to focus talent management and to identify emerging disruptive digitised processes), effective decision-making (to drive right strategic choices in a swift manner), and effective competitor analysis to sense any emerging disruptive threats so that proactive measures can be implemented.

Niche Model: Entails focusing on a profitable niche segment of the core market where disruption is limited owing to high capital barriers and the reliance on specialist capabilities. Executives will need capabilities in motivating, retaining and developing key talent required for maintaining market leadership in the niche segment. To deploy this business model effectively, executives will also need to develop collaborative capabilities that will enable them to work with selected competitors to maintain higher barriers of entry, as well as retain core customers and deepen customer experience.

Progressive digitisation: Involves gradual digitisation of operations across products and services, marketing and distribution channels, business processes, supply chains. Some of the capabilities that can assist executives in the successful delivery of this business model include, gaining the capacity to enhance cross-departmental collaboration to embed a digital mindset. Executives will also need to build on capabilities that will enable them to enhance the working relationships across the entire supply chain and also identifying and working with new partners situated within the broadening ecosystem (competitors, customers, regulators, governments, specialists, academics, etc), who may be critical for implementing a progressive digital model.

Disruption digital business models

Disrupt adjacent industries: Encompasses developing an entirely new business model, in an adjacent industry where it is possible to leverage existing knowledge and capabilities (e.g. Amazon to food retailing, IBM to consulting). Understanding the complementary and different capabilities required to operate effectively in adjacent industries, how to design an optimised organisation that fits this new model, how to transition from old to new models and the critical decision-making to ensure the speed of implementing new models will not negatively impact on existing structures, are some of the relevant capabilities that will be useful for executives in the successful deployment of this business model. Other capabilities that will be relevant to executives for the effective deployment of this model include understanding the key differences in the value drivers (existing versus target) and how these differences will impact on talent strategies and the capital structure of the combined portfolio.

Disrupt Current model: This revolves around creating new products, services and platforms to dilute the impact of disruptors, and leveraging inherent strengths to build the new business model (Uber to public transportation, Tesla into the automobile sector). Executives will need to develop start-up mentality, capacity to maintain an innovative culture, operate in flatter organisational structure where communication flow is frictionless (from bottom to top and vice versa), and the ability to build a culture of trust, openness, risk-taking and experimentation to deploy this business model effectively.

Aggressive digitisation: Requires fast-tracking the implementation of digital platforms to ensure a seamless interaction between customers in the co-creation, design, delivery of new products and to deepen the level of experience in existing product offerings. Cross-departmental collaboration, culture of openness and trust, encouraging integrative thinking across department and demolition of silo mentality and better prediction of and integration of customer needs into product development are some of the key capabilities that executives need to become adept at in order to deploy this model.

Disrupt in partnership with Ecosystem: Involves creating more compelling value propositions in new markets through connections with other companies to enhance the value available to the customer by improving customer experiences, collaborating more effectively with partners and driving ongoing innovation in products and services (Nike has collaborated with customers, external software developers, and hardware companies to build the digital fitness tracking innovation.) Apple Inc's idea of sharing the iPod on the Windows platform opened the iPod to Windows users and led to an explosive growth of the music player and the subsequent development of the iTunes Store, an ecosystem that would later contribute to the success of the iPhone.[16]

Chinese smartphone manufacturer Xiaomi is investing in Indian start-ups to speed up growth outside of its domestic market, by expanding the ecosystem of mobile apps to enhance customer experience, increase retention and accelerate market penetration. Xiaomi is building on the success of implementing this strategy in China; it has partnered with several different companies to propel the growth of the company within the local market.[17]

Executives need to develop the right capabilities to create an enabling environment for successful deployment of the ecosystem approach as it will involve working within a much broader bandwidth of external stakeholder groups and participants. This will include developing the capacity to connect with the right partners and link them to other leaders within their organisations, build effective collaborate relationships with all actors within the ecosystem, co-create profitable goods and services and consolidate market position and evaluate when to curtail the relationships. (All of these steps are depicted in Figure 1.5.)

Executives have to 'connect' with several leading and emerging businesses with capacity to disruption in adjacent and non-core business sectors as the first crucial step in implementing an ecosystem business model innovation. The number of partners needs be narrowed down to a few to ensure alignment with the strategic objectives of the collaboration. Stronger relationships have to be developed

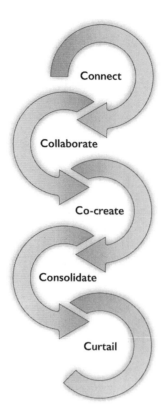

Figure 1.5 **Executive action for implementation of ecosystems business model innovation.**

to ensure that a 'collaborative' mindset can be established by building trusting relationships externally and concurrently enhance the internal teams' capacity to work within the ecosystem environment. Building an effective collaborative environment with ecosystems partners will lead to acceleration of 'co-creation' in terms of launching of disruptive products and services and integrating of unique features ideas into existing products to extend the customer value proposition.

For example, auto-maker Volvo is tapping into collaborating with Autoliv (a Swedish–American firm that makes automotive safety systems) to develop the necessary software, while a partnership with chip-maker Nvidia will supply the computing power in developing its autonomous driving technology.[18]

Consolidation of the business model will arise through forging a strong brand and developing complimentary products and services based on ecosystems and expanding into non-core business areas. It is important for executives to determine when to exit (curtail) the ecosystem before it becomes dilutive.

This requires executives to evaluate and exit non-profitable ecosystems platforms and create ones that align with the evolving organisational strategy. Operating within an ecosystem business model will also present a number of challenges such as working with multiple vendors and partners within an extended IT infrastructure, which can conflict with internal cybersecurity policies and data protection procedures. Revenue modelling, intellectual property and regulatory/compliance issues will call for executives to deploy effective negotiating skills to maximise the returns in investing in ecosystem business model innovation initiatives.

The fast tracking of digital business model innovation is a more intensive approach and require executives to develop a wider range of capabilities in order to embed digital technology and platforms in every dimension of the business operations to deliver better, faster, and enhanced customer experience and value. As this involves a reinvention of the operations, all levels of executives and organisational leaders need to acquire new capabilities to optimise decision making based on data analytics, cultivate and embed a digital culture and mindset, develop the digital talent pipeline across divisions and departments to deliver the cross functional initiatives required to improve and develop new offerings better than competitors to drive growth and embed value creation as a norm. The retailer, Marks & Spencer plc, seeking to accelerate the transition from a 'bricks and mortar' model to a digital business model, has launched a retail Data Academy in collaboration with Decoded (a technology education company) to provide senior executives from the board level to employees across all functions; retail, finance, marketing, customer service and operations with the expertise in machine learning, artificial intelligence and other areas necessary for transforming the digital behaviours, mindsets and cultures across all levels of the organisation to prepare it for the digital age.[19]

Executives will also need to develop capabilities required to shift the organisational culture towards a more ecosystem-friendly business model, as well as, determine how to set and track incisive success metrics for measuring the effectiveness of ecosystems relationships, create disruptive digital innovation models and to ensure that investment in such ventures can generate the intended benefits.[20]

In a nutshell, all the above pathways for digital business model innovation require executives to develop a range of capabilities to ensure maximisation of value and these need to be integrated into the development need analysis process, which is discussed in more detail in Chapter 4.

Customer retention and acquisition

Many organisations operate in mature segments where growth occurs at the expense of competitors. This makes the ability to retain customer very critical to growth; a study by Bain and Co indicates that a company's profitability can be enhanced by up to 75 per cent by a 5 per cent improvement in customer retention.[21] According to IBM customer relationship research, customers and companies have different perceptions about the impact of customer retention on profitability.[22] This misalignment in perception has implications on how organisations implement initiatives to retain and acquire new customers. More importantly, an Accenture research suggests that 80 per cent of an organisation's profit is normally derived from the top 20 per cent of customers (these are considered value-driving customers), whilst the bottom 30 per cent of the customer base destroy value and the middle 50 per cent bracket of customers are considered to be value-neutral.[23]

However, retention of the core 20 per cent customer base and concurrently attracting new customers is not an easy feat in an intensely competitive business landscape. The ability to retain these value-creating top customers requires executives to develop capabilities in a wide range of areas, including segmentation and targeting strategies, building stronger relationships with business units and sales teams and engaging in direct customer interactions and deep conversations to gain clear views of how customers use products and their preferences for the future. This also includes developing capabilities in social media, customer relationship management strategies and interpretation of data analytic outputs and predictive modelling to aid effective decision-making to drive retention strategies and interventions.

Strategic partnerships and alliances

Strategic alliances and partnerships in related and dissimilar industries as a means of developing new products and services is a common source of growth for companies. For example, the Google and Novartis partnership to develop a 'smart' contact lens to monitor sugar levels in the tears of diabetics has the potential to generate growth for both firms.

IBM and Apple have collaborated on several fronts in industry-specific enterprise software developed exclusively for iPhone and iPad. This provides a value-enhancing strategic alliance for both organisations as this venture generates revenue across several industries; see e.g. Boots (retail sector) and other clients including, Etisalat (telecom), Alior (banking), United Airlines and SAS (airline) and RWE (utility).[24]

ABB and Philips have also forged a partnership in commercial building automation services as a source of creating value for both organisations which will enable the two organisations to share complementary resources and generate long-term savings.[25]

In the automotive industry, Mazda, Denso and Toyota are dedicating an equal amount of development resources and taking advantage of existing production facilities to develop the basic structural technologies for Electric Vehicles to ensure rapid response to emerging market trends. This agreement combines the strengths of each company, including Mazda's bundled product planning and expertise in computer modelling-based development, Denso's electronics technologies, and the Toyota New Global Architecture (TNGA) platform.[26]

Another ambitious collaboration involves five auto-makers: Ford, Volkswagen, Audi, Porsche and Daimler joining forces to build a new high-power EV charging network across Europe, which will accommodate multiple brands of electric cars simultaneously, which in turn will require all executives involved to develop better collaborative capabilities and management of revenues generated by multiple partners.[27] This arrangement will also provide development opportunities for both senior managers and emerging talent from all the partnering organisation to gain experience in working effectively in an ecosystem environment.

Two global industrial automation and robot suppliers ABB and Kawasaki Heavy Industries are collaborating to share knowledge and promote the benefits of collaborative robots, while maintaining the independent manufacturing and marketing of their own offerings.[28]

To generate maximum benefits and value from strategic alliances and partnerships, executives need to expand their capabilities to include developing the diplomacy and gravitas to deal with challenging stakeholders, working collaboratively outside the normal span of control, effective negotiation of complex profit-sharing models and understanding of the legal boundaries and implications of working under such arrangements.

Mergers, acquisitions and asset swaps

Mergers and acquisitions (M&As) are a source of value creation but can equally result in value erosion if not managed effectively. Some of the drivers of value creation that arise from mergers and acquisitions include creation of synergy, market scale, elimination of market overlaps, utilisation of complementary assets, and improvement of bargaining power.[29]

Procter & Gamble's acquisition of Gillette led to a huge loss as it failed to generate the anticipated value. However, some M&A deals have been successful. Deals between Exxon and Mobil, Disney and Pixar, Shell and Royal Dutch Petroleum and J.P. Morgan and Chase are among the most successful. On the contrary, deals between Daimler/Chrysler, RBS/ABN Amro, AOL/Time Warner, News Corp/MySpace, Alcatel/Lucent and Nokia/Siemens Networks all failed to generate value. To increase the success rate of M&A activities, executives must develop capabilities across the whole spectrum of the M&A landscape: prospecting, targeting, deal valuation, culture alignment, integration and the post-integration phase activities necessary for creating value. Executives also need to assess their Leadership (executive) team bench strength, experience profiles and readiness to manage complexities of M&A activities so that any capability gaps can be closed. A track record of successful organic growth can serve as a good predicate for successful M&A activities. In a sample of 3,000 acquisitions by US companies from 2001 to 2011, only companies that generated robust organic growth created value (measured by total shareholder returns) from M&A activities. Executives of growing firms need to consolidate organic growth performance before venturing into M&A activities and allow sufficient time to build M&A capabilities across the executive bench before launching out into complex M&A campaigns.[30]

Asset swaps (involving the exchange of major assets by two companies) are emerging as an alternative strategy to M&As. The multibillion-dollar asset swap of nearly US$19 billion between GlaxoSmithKline and Novartis resulted in the former gaining the vaccine unit while it handed off its cancer treatment business to Novartis, providing a means of reducing some risks inherent in mergers and acquisitions.[31]

The GlaxoSmithKline/Novartis asset swap is expected to generate value because both companies are committed to playing to their strengths by building up certain businesses and divesting others while avoiding the pitfalls of large-scale mergers. However, asset swaps are not always risk-free. A proposed asset swap between BASF and Gazprom was scuppered initially owing to geo-political tensions but later on complete in 2015. The asset swap with BASF which gave Gazprom full control of jointly-operated European gas trading and storage businesses, including the biggest underground gas storage facility in Western Europe, was delayed owing to the consideration that the deal could pose a security threat to Germany.[32] But the deal, which was eventually consummated after two years' delay, offered BASF's Wintershall subsidiary a 25 per cent stake in the development and extraction of oil deposits in Russian Siberia, which enabled BASF to exit the gas trading and storage business to focus on oil and gas production.[33] This scenario amplifies why executives need to develop the right capabilities in assessing and evaluating possible geo-political uncertainties and risks that can impede the success of mergers and other business combinations such as asset swaps before committing resources and funds to such avenues.

Incremental and disruptive innovation

By balancing and blending incremental (core and adjacent) and disruptive (transformational) innovative initiatives, organisations can minimise the risks of excessive resource burnout on transformational innovation to fuel organic growth. In achieving this balance, some leading companies, including Google Microsoft and Apple, allocate around 70 per cent of their investment into core innovation initiatives (optimisation of existing offerings to enhance customer experience − least risk to investment return), 20 per cent to adjacent innovation projects (entering adjacent markets/customers by adding incremental features to existing offerings − reasonable risk to investment return) and 10 per cent to transformational innovation activities (developing disruptive new offerings targeted at new markets/customers − highest risk to investment return) and this approach enables such organisations to outperform their peers and carve a sustainable growth trajectory.[34] Clearly, these ratios and investment profiles in innovation cannot be applied carte blanche across industries but the innovation portfolio should be rebalanced to meet customer expectations, taking account of sector, geographic and other considerations and any gaps in capabilities required for delivering effective innovation need to be factored into executive development programmes. Several organisations such as Airbus, Siemens and Philips have embraced the open innovation approach by involving customers and other ecosystem partners. Airbus for instance, drives product innovation through engagement with airline executives, mechanics, pilots, passengers, and suppliers, which is supplemented by information gathered through annual customer needs analysis, and symposia with airlines to gauge evolving needs. Other channels pursued by Airbus to drive innovation include co-innovation workshops with airline customers to identify any industry trends and a portfolio of products to pursue to enhance end-to-end customer experience and value.[35] Executive capabilities needed to function effectively in this environment include; developing the capacity to network with the right partners (across several industries, sectors and backgrounds) and linking them to other leaders within their organisations, growing the initial collaborate relationships with all actors with the ecosystem, and developing effective communications skills to obtain relevant information from customers to create value-enhancing products.

Cost control and efficiencies

Embedding cost cutting and driving efficiencies are becoming integral to how organisations deliver their value proposition and improve profitability margins. Businesses in low-growth industries in the food and beverages sectors, such as Coca Cola, rely on aggressive efficiency programmes to deliver earnings growth. In the pharmaceutical sector, Novartis, for example, made productivity gains in one quarter alone to the tune of US$825 million (including US$400 million in procurement savings) in 2014. These improvements were driven through the company's productivity plans and aggressive cost reduction through portfolio restructuring and centralising of services.[36]

Maintaining the capacity to deliver efficiency savings consistently requires executives to deploy capabilities which will enable them to balance cost and value drivers, track benefits and engage the entire organisation in generating cost savings and embedding this as a norm as detailed in table 1.1.[1]

In addition to aligning organisational value-drivers with cost-cutting initiatives, it is imperative for executives to model the right behaviours to embed these cost reduction initiatives across the organisation. Executive development programmes need to focus on equipping the executive team to set the right tone at the top by demonstrating and reinforcing the right behaviours for employees to follow. Embedding a cost-cutting mindset within an organisation requires executives to deploy a range of capabilities, including advocacy, decisiveness, credibility and diplomacy.[37] These capabilities will

Table 1.1 Enablers and executive action required to embed a culture of efficiency and cost cutting programmes

Key Enablers	Required Executive Team Action / Capabilities
Map out cost drivers and explore alternative solutions	Identify all significant costs drivers, map out their sensitivity levels (top and bottom boundaries) and determine possible impact on profit margins. Rationalise all processes and parties within the internal / external supply chain and eliminate any redundant processes or replace with more efficient partners / processes. Establish the most significant cost drivers and identify any possible cheaper replacement / alternatives. Review opportunities to reduce complexities across products and processes. Locate any unidentified opportunities for economy of scale / scope, including standardisation of processes and products. Identify any low probability but high impact risks (including reputational risks) which can result in high costs implications. Identify and integrate any emerging technology, processes which can enhance customer value at lower cost. Identify any non-value adding / overlapping roles, departments and functions and eliminate / consolidate them.
Align cost cutting initiatives with value drivers	Map out and validate distinctive product / service features that drive the maximum customer value / experience and avoid cost cutting cost in these areas. Analyse the core features of services and products that customers want to retain and which ones are becoming obsolete and phase out the later. Target marketing initiatives to retain customer creating the maximum contribution to profitability.
Prioritise and balance for maximum outcome	Establish appropriate balance between cost and value across business units and product portfolios. Define and focus aspects of value drivers that need to be prioritised to achieve the maximum efficiency / cost reduction. Adapt governance process to support cross-organisational prioritisation of value drivers and cost reduction and eliminate any silo based approach. Allocate best resources and expertise to maximise value creating features and benefits of products and services.
Build cross departmental engagement and track benefits	Establish cross-departmental metrics for assessing cost-cutting effectiveness across business units, and divisions. Ensure that all departments and teams are aware of the benefits of cost reduction initiatives and are engaged, incentivised and motivated to drive the changes across the organisation. Automate and track levels of achievement of the cost reduction targets at the individual, team and departmental levels and build in trigger points for executive interventions and rewards.

help to send the right signals across the business to confirm executives' commitment to the cost reduction initiatives. Deploying these capabilities will remove any ambiguity and mixed messages to employees that executives are fully committed to the process by ruthlessly eliminating any behaviours and indications of maintaining certain perks for the 'privileged' club. For example, if a company announces a new travel policy as part of a cost cutting drive, executives must set the tone by aggressively using videoconferences instead of travelling first-class. Any mixed messages will dilute the commitment of employees to the cost saving process and hinder any progress in embedding efficiencies in the organisation. Executives also need to deploy diplomacy to secure peer support of inter-departmental/divisional commitment to drive a value-centric mindset across the organisation and ensure that non-value adding 'pet' projects are discontinued so that resources can be channelled appropriately. This requires political skills, effective stakeholder management (at peer-to-peer and lower levels) and the diplomacy to work behind the scenes to gain consensus across the organisation. Executives also need to deploy effective communication skills to provide clear examples and evidence of how value has been created through cost-cutting initiatives to build a critical mass and to consolidate any gains generated from such initiatives. Decisiveness and prompt action are also important capabilities required to ensure successful implementation of cost cutting initiatives, which need to be integrated into executive development programmes of organisations seeking to maximise the benefits of efficiency initiatives.

Executive development alignment with value and growth drivers

Executives who develop the right set of capabilities on a consistent basis build the capacity to challenge and change old paradigms and assumptions and replace these with new ones to influence the value and growth trajectory of their organisation. Acquiring new capabilities will result in empowering executives to lead their organisations in experimenting with new product launches, exploring new ways of understanding and meeting evolving customer needs, as well as taking measured risks to expand into new frontiers and markets. Effective development also allows executives in an organisation to strike an appropriate balance between the various initiatives needed to drive value and growth in the short, medium and long term. Executives' development plans need to be clearly aligned with the value-generating initiatives to motivate executives to imbibe new capabilities and identify opportunities to apply these capabilities to influence value and growth in the organisation. Alignment of executive development programmes/initiatives and value drivers offers an intrinsic motivation for executives by creating a mental connection between executive development and organisational outcomes which will be discussed in Chapters 6 and 7.

Creating an alignment between the executive development interventions and the target capabilities is required to drive value and the growth trajectory of the organisation which will be looked into more detail in future chapters. This will enable organisations to invest in development programmes which match the short-, medium- and long-term growth trajectory of the organisation, which will also provide a future-proof executive bench strength that can withstand any capability gaps that arise with the exit of any top executive member.

An organisation that has leveraged executive development to drive performance in the hospitality sector is Compass. Over an eight-year period (2006–2014), Compass Group, a food and support services catering firm, has delivered outstanding total shareholder return (TSR) growth.[38] Compass achieved this growth through a consistent and sustainable organic growth strategy which was supplemented by small to medium-sized infill acquisitions, adding both capability and scale in its existing markets. This successful growth rate is attributed to clear alignment of value drivers with executive and leadership development across the organisation, which was underpinned by the MAP framework. Implementation of the management and performance (MAP) framework which is aimed at articulating the value drivers (which enable Compass managers to share a common language across the international business) and is supported by intensive mapping-for-value customised leadership programmes for business leaders operating in different countries.[39] The programme helps to articulate and embed a common understanding of corporate value drivers, enables the rapid dissemination of best practices across the group and speeds the integration of acquisitions by creating rapid alignment of new businesses. Implementation of the MAP framework continues to be backed by a relentless focus on executive development and leadership development across the entire spectrum of the business. An example of this would be general managers and department heads looking for a new challenge engaging in the Evolve Programme, a leadership development programme which runs for 11 months and is supplemented by on-the-job learning and off-the-job training. Successful managers from Evolve can progress their careers as unit managers of some of Compass' largest and most complex operations. Compass also offers selected leaders true insight into senior leadership and development on a professional and personal level, shaping the leaders of the future through the INSights Management Programme/ Emerging Leaders Programme.[40] In summary, the MAP framework has been implemented successfully with the support of effective executive development, which is clearly aligned with organisational value drivers.

Similarly, Electrocomponents engineered a significant turnaround of its performance between 2012 and 2017 by deploying effective executive development and focusing on a sustainable growth business model. Matched against the historical five-year results, Electrocomponents' recent performance has been exceptional. It has achieved double-digit sales growth in a market battling the challenges of business digitalisation, supplier and OEM consolidation, rapid product introduction and obsolescence and swiftly changing customer demands.

The company's revenue strengthened by 17 per cent in 2017, compared to 2013.[41] To strengthen its commitment to developing leadership capabilities, the organisation has launched a new model of People Management to help build effective management skills. This focuses on three key 'habits' that create value: connect, perform and grow. In addition, a People Manager Academy programme has been developed. This helps equip managers with the mindset, skills and tools to get the best out of their people every day. The training is based on 'development bursts', in which training is compressed into action-packed 120-minute learning sessions full of tips and techniques.[42] The development mindset is extended to the director level where directors are encouraged to engage in both formal and informal development modalities to update and refresh their skills and knowledge by attending external seminars and briefings, visits to operating units, both in the UK and overseas, as well as by receiving presentations from senior management on emerging issues.

It is important to note that even when executive development programmes are aligned with value drivers, gaining the full commitment of executives to development programmes may be challenging and some of these barriers will be explored into more detailed in Chapter 3. But, in brief, it is worth highlighting some of these barriers which include the hyper busy schedule, short tenure and relatively small number of executive cohorts spanning the organisational hierarchy. These factors, which can constrain the capacity for executives to develop, apply and transfer capabilities to create an enabling environment, prioritise value-driving initiatives and align these initiatives to the organisational architecture to generate value and growth. These unique features of executives need to be accounted for in the process of designing and implementing executive development programmes to maximise the return on investment and this will be discussed into more depth in Chapter 3.

In conclusion, it is important to highlight that the alignment of executive development programmes with value drivers does not only offer an intrinsic motivation for executives to remain committed in spite of their busy schedules (by creating a mental connection between executive development and organisational outcomes) but also provides a solid foundation for developing the metrics that are employed to assess the impact of such interventions on organisational performance.

Summary of key points

The VUCA environment, digital disruptions, ever-shifting customer expectations and uncontrollable events such as natural disasters, epidemics and geo-political tensions is making the prediction of future profitability almost impossible.

The combined effect of these factors is affecting the capacity for organisations to create consistent value and financial growth and therefore executives need to be expanding their capabilities on a more frequent basis to prepare for emerging business challenges.

Executives need to recognise that developing and swift application of new capabilities is a new currency for driving organisational survival. It also provides the capacity for executives to adapt quickly in uncertain times and lay the foundation for long-term organisational growth.

Organisations can generally create value and growth under two broad categories, organic growth and/or business combination and partnerships initiatives.

However, the successful implementation of these initiatives requires executives to exhibit certain unique capabilities at the individual and team level. These unique capabilities must be harnessed consistently to create an enabling environment for employees to innovate and improve productivity levels.

Executives also need to deploy these capabilities to align the overall organisational architecture (a nexus of processes, technology, culture and values) to drive customer-centric innovation in the short-term and at the same time prepare for emerging trends (including mega events) that can disrupt existing business models. This will be explored into detail in Chapter 5.

The role of executive development in creating value needs to be embedded within the entire fabric of an organisation.

Executive development must improve the functional deficiencies of individual executives and enable them to exert their full potential for the benefit of the organisation. It must also stimulate the capabilities of the entire executive cohort, as well as individual needs. in group interactions and interventions.

Executives who develop the right set of capabilities on a consistent basis build the capacity to challenge and change old paradigms and assumptions and replace these with new ones to influence the value and growth trajectory of their organisation. This will position the organisation to strike an appropriate balance between the various initiatives needed to drive value and growth in the short, medium and long term.

Executive development plans need to be clearly aligned with the value- and growth-generating initiatives to motivate executives to imbibe new capabilities and identify opportunities to apply these capabilities to influence value and growth in the organisation.

Executive development initiatives must be actively deployed as a means of equipping executives to prevent organisational decline, prepare the organisation for external threats and to futureproof the organisation in the face of the emerging digital revolution, automation, artificial intelligence and the plethora of changes which will transform the business landscape to an unrecognisable level.

Organisations who intentionally embed executive learning into its fabric strand a better chance of surviving in this new era of constant change because they will become more proactive instead of being reactive to disruptions and trends and adjust their business models ahead of competitors.

Note

1   Ideas for the Key Enablers in Table 1.1 were derived from the following source: PricewaterhouseCoopers, 'Leader or follower? The role of the CFO in cost reduction' (PwC 2009) https://www.pwc.co.uk/assets/pdf/0900409-cfo-in-cost-reduction-brochurev7jt.pdf (last accessed 20 November 2016).

References

1. Xandra Chang Gear, '5 Reasons why Nokia lost its handset sales and got downgraded to 'junk'' (*Wired*, 5 April 2012) https://www.wired.com/2012/04/5-reasons-why-nokia-lost-its-handset-sales-lead-and-got-downgraded-to-junk/ (last accessed 20 November 2016).
2. Yves Doz, 'The Strategic Decisions That Caused Nokia's Failure' (Insead Knowledge, 23 November 2017) https://knowledge.insead.edu/strategy/the-strategic-decisions-that-caused-nokias-failure7766 (last accessed 30 November 2017).
3. Harvey Schachter, 'Lessons learned from Kodak's collapse' (*The Globe and Mail*, 29 January 2012, updated 26 March 2017) https://www.theglobeandmail.com/report-on-business/careers/management/lessons-learned-from-kodaks-collapse/article621179/ (last accessed 31 November 2017).
4. Rosemount Hutt, 'Why have commodities crashed?' (*World Economic Forum*, 11 December 2015) https://www.weforum.org/agenda/2015/12/why-have-commodities-crashed/ (last accessed 31 November 2017).
5. Jon Yeomans, 'Lonmin agrees 285m takeover by Sibanye-Stillwater' (*The Telegraph*, 14 December 2017) https://www.telegraph.co.uk/business/2017/12/14/lonmin-agrees-285m-takeover-sibanye-stillwater/ (last accessed 20 December 2017).
6. Thomas R. Robinson, Elaine Henry, Wendy L. Pirie, Michael A. Broihahn and Anthony T. Cope, *International Financial Statement Analysis* (3rd edn, Wiley 2015) 344.
7. Nathaniel J. Mass, 'The Relative Value of Growth' (*Harvard Business Review*, April 2005 Issue) https://hbr.org/2005/04/the-relative-value-of-growth (last accessed 20 March 2016).
8. Gary L. Neilson and Julie Wulf, 'How many Direct Reports?' (*Harvard Business Review*, April 2012) https://hbr.org/2012/04/how-many-direct-reports (last accessed 20 November 2017).
9. Stephanie Overby, 'Meet the New Chief Growth Officer' (*CMO*, 10 July 2017) http://www.cmo.com/features/articles/2017/6/12/six-steps-to-owning-the-growth-agenda.html#gs.kvmb3lc (last accessed 21 November 2017).
10. Chris Pierce, *The Effective Director* (Kogan Page 2001).
11. Ian Beardwell and Len Holden, *Human Resource Management: A Contemporary Approach* (3rd edn Pearson Education 2001).
12. Solomon Akrofi, 'Evaluating the effects of executive learning and development on organisational performance: implications for developing senior manager and executive capabilities' (2016) 20(3) *International Journal of Training and Development* 177.
13. Ron Carucci, 'A-10-year-study-reveals-what-great-executives-know-and-do' (*Harvard Business Review*, 19 January 2016) https://hbr.org/2016/01/a-10-year-study-reveals-what-great-executives-know-and-do (last accessed 23 November 2017).

14. Richard L. Daft, *Management* (CENGAGE Learning 2015) 258.

15. Cassandra Frangos, 'How Cisco Gets Brutally Honest Feedback to Top Leaders' (*Harvard Business Review*, 29 December 2015) https://hbr.org/2015/12/how-cisco-gets-brutally-honest-feedback-to-top-leaders (last accessed 23 November 2017).

16. Drake Baer, 'Here's what Apple Teaches Employees in Its Ultra-Secretive Internal Training Program' (*Business Insider* 13 August 2016) http://www.business insider.com/what-apple-teaches-in-secret-training-program-2014-8?IR=T (last accessed 23 November 2017).

17. Meha Agarwal, 'Xiaomi to Invest US$1 Bn in 100 Indian Startups: CEO Lei Jun; Xiaomi Will Invest US$1 Bn Over the Next 5 Years with Aim to Create Ecosystem of Apps Around Its Smartphone Brand' (*Inc42* 20 November 2017) https://inc42.com/buzz/xiaomi-indian-startups-lei-jun/ (last accessed 23 November 2017).

18. Andrew J. Hawkins, 'Volvo is reportedly scaling back its ambitious self-driving car experiment – The automaker had planned to deliver 100 autonomous SUVs to families in Sweden, China, and the UK' (*The Verge* 14 December 2017) https://www.theverge.com/platform/amp/2017/12/14/16776466/volvo-drive-me-self-driving-car-sweden-delay (last accessed 30 December 2017).

19. Ellen Hammett, 'M&S sets up data academy to turn staff into data scientists' (*Marketing Week* 30 Jul 2018) https://www.marketingweek.com/2018/07/30/marks-spencer-data-academy/ (last accessed 30 July 2018).

20. Reinhard Geissbauer, Jesper Vedso and Stefan Schrauf, 'Industries 4.0 Building your digital enterprise' (PwC 2016) https://www.pwc.com/gx/en/industries/industries-4.0/landing-page/industry-4.0-building-your-digital-enterprise-april-2016.pdf (last accessed 30 December 2017).

21. C. H. Baird and G. Parasnis, 'From social media to social CRM, Reinventing the customer relationship' (IBM Institute for Business Value 2011) https://www.ibm.com/midmarket/uk/en/att/pdf/social_media_Part_Executive_Report.pdf> (last accessed 23 November 2017).

22. ibid.

23. Donniel Schulman, Kris Timmeermans, Kim De Maeseneer and Robert Willems, 'Increasing agility to fuel growth and competitiveness' (Accenture 2016) https://www.accenture.com/_acnmedia/Accenture/Conversion-Assets/DotCom/Documents/Global/PDF/Dualpub_24/AccentureConsulting-Increasing-Agility-to-Fuel-Growth-and-Competitiveness.pdf (last accessed 3 December 2017).

24. Apple Press Release, 'Apple and IBM Forge Global Partnership to Transform Enterprise Mobility' (Apple 15 July 2014) https://www.apple.com/uk/newsroom/2014/07/15Apple-and-IBM-Forge-Global-Partnership-to-Transform-Enterprise-Mobility/ (last accessed 5 December 2017).

25. Philips Press Release, 'ABB and Philips join forces in commercial building automation for energy efficiency and increased functionality' (Philips 31 March 2014) https://www.philips.com/a-w/about/news/archive/standard/news/press/2014/20140331-ABB-and-Philips-join-forces-in-commercial-building-automation-for-energy-efficiency-and-increased-functionality.html (last accessed 5 December 2016).

26. Toyota News Release, 'Mazda, Denso, and Toyota Sign Joint Technology Development Contract for Electric Vehicles' (Toyota, 28 September 2017) http://

corporatenews.pressroom.toyota.com/releases/mazda+denso+toyota+sign+joint+technology+development+contract+electric+vehicles.htm (last accessed 20 November 2017).

27. Mark Austin, 'Automakers unite to create an electric vehicle charging network across Europe' (*Digital Trends*, 5 November 2017) https://www.digitaltrends.com/cars/ionity-european-charging-station-partnership/amp/ (last accessed 21 November 2017).

28. ABB, 'ABB and Kawasaki announce collaborative robot automation cooperation' (ABB Group Press Release, 27 November 2017) http://new.abb.com/news/detail/2585/abb-and-kawasaki-announce-collaborative-robot-automation-cooperation (last accessed 1 December 2017).

29. Sydney Finkelstein, and Cary L. Cooper, *Advances in Mergers and Acquisitions* (Emerald Group Publishing 2010) 127.

30. Ken Favaro, David Meer and Samrat Sharma, 'Creating an Organic Growth Machine' (Harvard Business Review, May 2012) https://hbr.org/2012/05/creating-an-organic-growth-machine (last accessed 30 November 2016).

31. *The Telegraph*, 'GSK and Novartis complete deals to reshape both drugmakers' (2 March 2015) http://www.telegraph.co.uk/finance/newsbysector/pharmaceuticalsandchemicals/11444023/GSK-and-Novartis-complete-deals-to-reshape-both-drugmakers.html (last accessed 20 November 2016).

32. Simone Tagliapietra, *Energy Relations in the Euro-Mediterranean: A Political Economy Perspective* (Springer 2016) 53.

33. BASF Group, 'BASF and Gazprom agree to complete asset swap' (*BASF Business & Financial News* 4 September 2015) https://www.basf.com/en/company/news-and-media/news-releases/2015/09/p-15-330.html (last accessed 20 November 2016).

34. Bansi Nagji and Geoff Tuff, 'Managing your innovation portfolio' (Harvard Business Review May 2012) https://hbr.org/2012/05/managing-your-innovation-portfolio (last accessed 21 November 2016).

35. Steven Melendez, 'Airbus exec on co-innovation and seizing opportunities outside the airplane' (*Innovation Insider* 14 March 2016) https://www.innovationleader.com/airbus-exec-co-innovation-seizing-opportunities-outside-airplane/ (last accessed 21 November 2017).

36. Novartis International AG, '2015 Financial Results' (Novartis 2015) https://www.novartis.com/sites/www.novartis.com/files/q4-2015-media-release-en.pdf (last accessed 12 November 2016).

37. PricewaterhouseCoopers, 'Leader or follower? The role of the CFO in cost reduction' (PwC 2009) https://www.pwc.co.uk/assets/pdf/0900409-cfo-in-cost-reduction-brochurev7jt.pdf (last accessed 20 November 2016).

38. Compass Group, 'Annual Results 2015' (Compass Group Press Release 24 November 2015) https://www.compass-group.com/content/dam/compass-group/corporate/Investors/Results-presentations/2015/FullYearResults/151124_FY_15_Press_Release.pdf.downloadasset.pdf (last accessed 23 November 2016).

39. Compass Group, Strategy and Business Model (Compass Group) https://www.compass-group.com/en/who-we-are/strategy-and-business-model.html (last accessed 23 November 2016).

40. Kim Shanahan, 'Interview with Gary Snyder, Chief People Officer, Compass Group North America' (*AccelHRate HRO Magazine* 5 January 2015) http://www.accelhrate.com/interview-gary-snyder-chief-people-officer-compass-group-north-america/ (last accessed 23 November 2016).
41. Electrocomponents PLC, 'Annual Report and Accounts 2013' (Electrocomponents PLC, 2014) http://www.electrocomponents.com/~/media/Files/E/ElectroComponents/documents/reports-presentations/reports/electrocomponents-annual-report-2013.pdf (last accessed 30 December 2017).
42. Electrocomponents PLC, 'Annual Report and Accounts 2017' (Electrocomponents PLC, 2017) http://www.electrocomponents.com/~/media/Files/E/ElectroComponents/documents/annual-reports/2017/electrocomponents-annual-report-2017.pdf (last accessed 30 December 2017).

2

Mapping out value-centric executive capabilities

The crucial connection between executive development capabilities and business value and growth which was introduced in chapter one is expanded here by mapping specific capabilities to drivers of successful organic growth, M&A and a hybrid of the two approaches. A study conducted by Egon Zehnder International and McKinsey and Company indicates that companies pursuing hybrid growth strategies (acquisition and organic) rely on a range of executive capabilities encompassing customer impact, market insight, result orientation, change leadership, team leadership, collaboration, influencing and strategic orientation.[1]

Comparing high- and low-performing 47 listed organisations across the services and industrial sectors, the study highlights further the need for organisations to equip top executives adequately for M&A activities, as this requires the deployment of a broad range of capabilities to minimise value dilution. Thus, large organisations seeking to generate greater value and growth from M&A activities can broaden their development programmes to enhance executives' ability to challenge assumptions related to all the eight identified capabilities. However, the repertoire of capabilities identified within the Egon Zehnder International and McKinsey & Company study are limited in the sense that most of the capabilities, apart from market insight, focus on generating short-term impact and fail to address long-term sustainable growth. This limitation can be addressed by augmenting these capabilities with others, which can enable executives to predict future trends and adapt the organisational structure, culture and values to benefit from future events. The importance of gaining the capacity to predict future trends and events is becoming more crucial owing to the rapid advancements in both artificial intelligence and automation and the impact these are having on business models and industry norms and practices.

The future of human-machine collaboration and its impact on the workplace – and how this feature can be enhanced to deliver value and long-term growth – needs to be given consideration by executives. Executives will need to identify the systems, processes and roles to automate whilst determining which elements are to be undertaken by employees. This also means identifying new roles and combining some in order to drive productivity, innovation and customer-centric products and services by leveraging the benefits of artificial intelligence and automation. For instance, artificial intelligence has the potential of transforming all aspects of the financial services industry with the introduction of robo-advisory, predictive budgeting, intelligent market tracking, chat boxes and other emerging machine learning based technology which will revolutionise the entire sector within the next few decades.

Enhanced preparedness for future events enables executives to deploy strategic insight and execution capabilities to drive value and growth that aligns within the short-term and concurrently prepare for long-term events that can impact on the survival of the organisation. Sharper execution capabilities can enable organisations to produce unique products in a timely manner to meet the needs of customers in both mature and emerging markets. At the same time, execution speed facilitates rapid conversion of opportunities or address threats by enabling executives to restructure the organisational architecture to tap into emerging/future opportunities ahead of competitors, which contributes toward generating sustainable growth. Strategic insight enables executives to anticipate changes in customer profiles, technological trends, the competition landscape and regulation. In the UK retail grocery sector, for example, some executives failed to grasp the speed of the digital transformation in the business landscape, which rendered the approach of expanding through space and megastores (pursued by large UK retailers such as Tesco, Sainsbury and Morrisons) obsolete. Customer behaviour is shifting toward greater value and swift delivery and is also embracing the greater appeal of discounting retailers (for example, the success of Lidl and Aldi in other European markets), which has taken many incumbents in this sector by surprise. This exemplifies the need for executives to acquire a range of capabilities that equip them with strategic insight into how to evolve their business models and balance this with strong execution capabilities to achieve value and growth. This resonates with the points made in Chapter 1 on the 'lack of ability to adapt quickly to the changing horizons within the business environment which can impact on organisational growth prospects'.

UK fashion retailer, Oasis has mastered the omni-channel/multi-channel sales model to recover from loss-making and bucked the trend in the decline in sales faced by others within that sector.[2] The omni-channel approach has allowed the retailer to provide the customer with a seamless integrated shopping experience by providing the platform to shop online from a desktop or mobile device, or by telephone, or in a bricks and mortar store. This then aids in generating long-term customer loyalty and profitability. To implement the omni-channel model effectively, retailers need to have a roadmap of digital marketing and channel integration initiatives built on a sound understanding of customer behaviour. This requires executives to have solid capabilities in data analytics in order to target, differentiate and deliver customised and integrated omni-channel experiences to delight customers. Retail executives and others within service sector organisations can benefit from embedding the omni-channel model into their core business models, rather than bolting it onto existing practices, in order to unlock the benefits from multiple customer touchpoints.

These cases in the retail sector exemplify the need for executives to become more adept at acquiring the capabilities necessary for harnessing strategic insight to evolve their business models, as well as the execution speed required to achieve consistent value and growth. An organisation that can inculcate this approach within its executive cohort will remain relevant in a constantly changing marketplace and will build the resilience to survive and grow in a future environment, where customer loyalty is based on offering value-added services and products rather than on blind loyalty to big brands.

Executive development programmes and solutions should also include features that equip executives with capabilities that sharpen their ability to predict future events and mega trends. This will allow executives to prepare for future events and invest in business initiatives that can generate value and assure sustainable growth in the short and long term. Five major trends expected to materialise by 2030 have an impact on the leadership styles that executives will need to deploy in the future.[3] The predicted trends include intensive globalisation, individualism, digitisation, demographic changes and technology convergence. Globalisation trends are likely to shift, with Asia predicted to occupy a dominant space in the global economy which will mean that organisations operating outside these regions will need to adapt their offerings to customers with the different demographics, cultures, behaviours and preferences, whilst meeting the demands of existing markets. This will call for new capabilities across all levels in the organisation and more crucially for executives in their decision-making capabilities to assess how to exit legacy markets, manage transition into new markets (including managing geopolitical risks) and how to achieve the right balance across the business portfolio to maximise value and growth. Greater shifts towards individualism imply that people have more freedom of choice, which erodes loyalty and employee motivation and requires different leadership responses from executives to address challenges from an inter-generational and diverse workforce. Digitisation is also likely to drive work environments to mobile spaces and the boundaries will blur between private and professional life. Demographic changes such as aging populations will intensify talent wars as millennials compete with the older generation for top positions and this requires executives to be adept at managing inter-generational leadership teams, deconflicting any possible tensions in values and cultural norms to ensure that the workplace environment is conducive for employees to excel in their daily activities. Technology convergence will also lead to the emergence of powerful new technology, which will transform many aspects of everyday life. The effects of semi-autonomous technologies, robots and transportation on value creation are also areas that warrant executives' attention and action.

The insurance firm Legal and General (L&G) has been proactive and already started benefiting from these trends, consistently by generating solid operating profits in a tough competitive landscape. L&G has shrunk its size to half of what it was a decade ago and positioned itself for growth by focusing its business around five key themes – aging populations, globalisation of asset markets, creation of real physical assets, welfare reforms and digital lifestyles (revolution).[4]

These trends will cause executives to move more frequently across sectors and industries, rely less on technical and task-oriented capabilities and focus more on developing people-centric leadership capabilities to operate across sectors. Executives will have to adopt a more personable approach to leadership and deploy emotional intelligence to identify employee strengths and provide them with opportunities that align with creating value and achieving organisational goals. This requires executives to develop the capability to zoom in on individuals to get the best out of them and zoom out of task and details to allow bottom-up innovation and creativity to emerge more regularly from the workforce. Collaboration will not only involve working across disciplines and departments but also with people from different cultural backgrounds, particularly as the workforce becomes more diverse in terms of age, values and demographic make-up. Diversity management will be one of the top items on the leadership agenda. Executives must be prepared for these future challenges through effective development programmes that address the quantum shift from the traditional command-and-control management and leadership styles to one that is aligned with employees' shift towards a semi-autonomous mode with less intrusion. Diversity management will be a key area of development for executives which will provoke a mentality of 'listening' more and engaging with a diverse group of people (internally and externally), generating perspectives from different areas of the business which will lead to more pluralistic decision-making with positive outcomes. As mentioned in Chapter 1, the shift towards ecosystem business models will transform the cultural and operational boundaries of organisations seeking to provide customised and innovative products to customers. Executives will therefore need to develop strategic capabilities to launch disruptive business models through ecosystem platforms as well as aligning the internal organisational structures, systems, values, culture to the ecosystem approach whilst continuing to build 'existing' business models.

Capabilities that executives need to develop to achieve specific value drivers and growth (referenced in Chapter 1 – Customer Retention, Innovation, Business Model Innovation) in the short, medium and long-term are summarised in Table 2.1. These have been derived by expanding the eight capabilities identified and introduced at the beginning of this chapter(customer impact, market insight, result orientation, change leadership, team leadership,

Table 2.1 Summary of value-generating executive capabilities

Executive Capability	Description	Value driver
Result Driven	**Customer Impact** – Manage customer acquisition, retention and lifetime value.	**Customer retention**
Result Driven	**Results Orientation** – Drive for higher performance across business units and operations.	**Enabler of growth**
Result Driven	**Change Leadership** – Champions and drives efficient delivery of innovation and change initiatives.	**Innovation**
Result Driven	**Strategic Orientation** – Effective implementation of strategy and clear definition of strategy into tangible steps across business units / divisions.	**Enabler of growth**
Results Driven	**Business model maximisation** – Creating and capturing value by rethinking value propositions, identifying unmet customer needs and re-structuring business models.	**Business model maximisation**
Results Driven	**Merger and acquisition insight** – Strategic acquisitions and mergers to generate value and growth.	**Enabler of growth**
Results Driven	**External networking capabilities** – Effective networking outside organisation to spot trends and opportunities to drive internal organisational growth.	**Strategic partnerships and alliances**
Results driven	**Decision-making** – Making effective decisions to seize opportunities to drive value and growth.	**Enabler of growth**
Future-centric	**Future orientation** – Preparing for the challenges of technological convergence and demographic changes in the workforce. Includes preparing for automation, artificial intelligence and digital disruptions.	**Innovation / customer retention**
Future-centric	**Predicting future customer needs** – Predicting customer needs through analytics, machine and deep leaning, social media and intelligent research.	**Customer retention**
Future-centric	**Market insight** – Looking beyond current context and predicting new customer needs.	**Innovation / customer retention**
People-centric	**Team leadership** – Cross-functional collaboration and influence to drive innovation and problem solving.	**Innovation**
People-centric	**Ethical and emotional intelligence** – Reflection on behaviours and demonstrating and promoting ethical conduct and integrity.	**Enabler of growth**
People-centric	**Inclusiveness** – Building a culture that embraces professionalism, diversity, and celebrates the uniqueness of individuals.	**Enabler of growth**

collaboration, influencing and strategic orientation) to encompass other ones (such as business model optimisation, external networking, decision-making, future-orientation, predicting customer needs, ethical and emotional intelligence and inclusiveness), which can prepare executives to predict future trends and adapt the organisational structure, culture and values to benefit from future events.

Most of the value-generating executive capabilities listed in Table 2 map directly to the organic and combination value drivers outlined in Chapter 1. For example, developing a compelling customer impact capability results in greater customer retention and likewise maintaining future orientation can drive greater innovation focus.

Other capabilities such as decision-making, inclusiveness and ethical and emotional intelligence have a more indirect connection to the generation of value but are important in maintaining long-term and sustainable growth. Team leadership at the executive and direct report level is important as it helps to drive deeper cross-functional collaboration and can influence innovation and problem solving and place the organisation in a strong position to deliver value-centric products and services. Similarly, external networking capabilities can enable executives to spot trends and acquire information which can be employed to change organisational culture, launch new products and initiate strategic collaborations and partnerships, all of which can contribute towards an enhanced organisational value. Driving a sense of inclusiveness is another important capability that executives can utilise to build a culture that embraces professionalism and diversity, so that employees can be motivated to contribute towards organisational objectives.

Result driven capabilities

Customer impact: – managing customer acquisition, retention and lifetime value in the digital economy will require organisations to provide a seamless and connected experience. This will require understanding the changing customer ecosystem by using tools and techniques such as customer journey mapping, emotion modelling, customer future-casting, and persona profiling to provide organisations insights necessary for creating and delivering unique experiences throughout the entire customer lifecycle. The speed of the end to end customer experience journey is shortening owing to the power of Artificial Intelligence. For example, IBM Watson Ads are speeding up product innovation and creating personalised offers using real-time customer feedback.[5] North Face, the clothing retailer provides a platform for consumers to customise clothing, based on variables like location and gender preference based on IBM Watson's cognitive computing technology.[6]

Toyota is also leveraging the AI powered IBM Watson Ad platform to engage and educate consumers about new and existing products, address consumer questions, share information and offer guidance on purchase decisions, whilst concurrently gaining actionable data and insights about consumer preferences, non-intuitive behaviours patterns and emerging trends.[7]

Other organisations such as Alibaba, Amazon, Cisco, Lush, Lexus, Nubank, Starbucks, Uber and Zurich Insurance are strategically using AI to create compelling, convenient, and intimate experiences to acquire, retain and consolidate their customer base in order to maintain and grow their market positions.[8]

At Cisco, data automation and analytics is being employed to identify user utilisation patterns, product and service lifecycles and digital touchpoints across its product portfolios. This will enable the company to deliver enhanced personalisation to its partners and drive value for the organisation.[9]

Lexus in partnership with Xevo (an automotive software supplier) and Voicebox Technologies (Voice Recognition & Language Understanding software supplier) have developed AI platforms which provide an interactive in-car experience allowing drivers to safely interact with their car's mobile services and applications, creating a unified voice interface between both devices.[10] This offering appeals to urban customer with busy lifestyles seeking for features which will make their daily commute more productive but also provide valuable predictive data which can feed into future product development.

Similarly, Zurich Insurance has embedded AI in the form of cognitive automation into its personal injury claims operations, which resulted in improvements in customer experience and claims-processing consistency, with significant reduction in claims processing operational costs.[11]

The Korean automobile maker Kia motors, has developed a chatbox dubbed 'Kian', which integrates artificial intelligence and machine learning to provide an analytical interface which helps to identify how specific groups of customer exhibit behaviours in order to allow personalisation and better engagement for customers.[12] The platform also serves as an intuitive medium where all question regarding purchasing and after sales support can be offered and has helped to increase the sales conversion rate by three fold compared to previous customer reliance on basic website information.

The ability to create effective customer insight does not only require executives to focus on deploying data and technological tools but, more importantly on developing the capacity to empower front-line employees to deepen customer experiences and build intimacy to generate long-term value.

Apple, Nordstrom, Intuit, Ritz-Carlton Hotel Company, Southwest Airlines, Starbucks and Zappos, and many other organisations are creating distinctive experiences by coaching and empowering employees to create positive emotional connections with customers, which in turn generates customer loyalty and return custom.[13]

Combining technological capabilities from AI and building stronger customer intimacy to provide customisation and unique product is a winning formula. This requires executive to develop the right capabilities which can enable them to create an open, flexible and customer-driven culture where employees are not only empowered to deliver exceptional customer service but also the reward mechanisms are connected to delivery of customer loyalty metrics.[14]

Results orientation: Result oriented mindsets and capabilities must not be pursued at the expense of ethical values, which is one of the people-centric capabilities which is discussed later on in this chapter and executives should also avoid the aggressive behaviours that were systematically embedded in organisations such as Enron as this can result in organisational failure.[15] To avoid falling into this trap of pursuing success at all cost, executives need to engage in reflective practice and coaching at the individual and team levels to ensure that a balanced approach is taken toward achieving result orientation which takes into account a strong ethical mindset without sacrificing long-term gains for short-term profits.

Change leadership: Executives need to develop the capabilities to champion and drive an effective change culture and an environment where difficult conversations can take place, where risk-taking is promoted, and cross-functional teams can work effectively to build a cohesive and communicative environment and eventually feed into the organisational culture.[16] Such an environment will engender shared ideas to challenge the status quo, generate innovative thinking and products and services which will enhance customer experiences.

Strategic orientation: Effective implementation of strategy and clear definition of strategy into tangible steps across business units/divisions can be very challenging owing to competing agendas which may exist within divisions and lower levels within organisations. Executives can use deep-dive exercises, regular site visits and experiential learning modalities to unearth these competing agendas and other obstacles which can derail the effective implementation of strategic initiatives.

Business model maximisation: Creating and capturing value by rethinking value propositions, identifying unmet customer needs and re-structuring business models will require executives to be adept at combining customer insight gleaned from customer journey mapping, emotion modelling, customer future-casting (understanding the profile of future customers, their preferences, behaviours, personas, etc in order to better position offerings to suit them), demographic profiling coupled with pricing, revenue and scenario modelling to determine when to enter and exit certain markets or business portfolios. Gamification, competitor analysis, value-chain analysis and short courses in micro-economics, as well as learning from start-up entrepreneurs are some of the useful modalities for expanding executives' capabilities to maximise existing business models and to plan for the next disruptive business models.

Merger and acquisition insight: Executives with mergers and acquisition insight can improve the chances of successful business combination interventions. The right set of capabilities can be leveraged to address some of the inherent risks of M&A strategies (referenced in Chapter 1). Executives can expand these capabilities through decision-based gamification, exposure to diverse board level experiences in other sectors, and tapping into networks for advice. Some of the areas that can be enhanced through the development process includes better identification of value drivers – regulatory, competitor, operational and financial factors which can result in failure of the business combination strategy. Early identification of the value drivers of the M&A activity can result in pursuing an organic growth strategy instead of following a dilutive M&A approach. Executives involved in M&A activities may need analytical capabilities to conduct what-if analyses (including fact-based evaluations of alternative business models and risk-specific scenarios), cultural compatibility tests and pre-empting of post-merger challenges, which can derail the intended benefits of the business combination, in order to identify the correct value drivers that need to be changed to propel organic growth instead of a dilutive acquisition.

External networking capabilities: Executives can leverage external networking as a support mechanism to address isolationist effects and can also use it as a mechanism to spot trends, challenge any unconsciousness biases that may exist within the top teams and, more importantly, identify any opportunities in non-core industries that can be deployed to drive organisational growth. A strong internal networking capability is also a vital source for gaining support, feedback, insight, resources, and information for executives at all levels in their career. It also helps break cross-functional barriers that can stifle the successful deployment of innovative solutions.

CEMEX, the global building materials giant, recognises the importance of networking and embeds this capability within the top executive cohort via global leadership networks to promote information sharing, collaboration, and dissemination of best practices. Strong network principles have been integrated into the company's approach to the design of leadership development processes with opportunities for connecting the top executive team, direct reports, and high-potential pool with further avenues for interaction available via a social collaboration platform called *Shift*.[17]

Well-developed internal networking capabilities can be used to remove cross-functional barriers to accelerate innovation and creativity, cascade informal learning and generate innovative ideas and is a crucial avenue for locating talent and critical resources required for delivering special projects within short timescales. Similarly, external networking is beneficial in identifying sector trends and emerging technologies, locating contacts for building strategic partnerships and successful business ecosystem business models, identifying effective executive coaching experts based on experience of peers within the wider network and a source for challenging internal biases and group-think within the executive team.

Executives need to learn how to build internal and external connections, expand this network, and re-orient the network as they progress in seniority.

A director appointed to a foreign market may need coaching support to expand their networking with politicians and other stakeholders with higher power and authority to navigate challenges which can lead to reputational damage to the organisation. As this director gains traction in the new market, she may need further support to expand the span of her network to encompass key customers and brand ambassadors to understand how the organisation's offerings can be localised to gain loyalty.

Decision-making

Decisiveness has been identified as one of the key capabilities that successful CEOs need to exhibit to survive in the digital economy and situations of uncertainty.[18]

Most decisions made by executives are usually complex and involve exploring new terrain and interaction of various sources of information to arrive at an optimum outcome. This often requires executives to engage in reflection, deep probing, and experimentation to locate a range of solutions before an appropriate response can be formulated.[19]

Furthermore, executive decision-makers may have the tendency or propensity to default into one of five primary modes of charismatics, thinkers, specifics, followers and controllers[20] as summarised below and depending on the composition of the team, these characteristics can skew decisions in a particular direction:

Charismatic – embrace ideas with excitement but final decisions and judgements are derived by consideration of a balanced set of information and sources.

Thinkers – articulate contradictory points of view and cautiously work through options before making a final decision.

Sceptics – harbour suspicions regarding information that does not align with their worldview and make decisions based on their gut feelings.

Followers – make decisions based on how other trusted executives have acted or recollection/experience of similar decisions made in the past.

Controllers – focus on pure facts and analysis of decisions because of their own fears and uncertainties.

Whilst all executives may have a default style, the decision-making process will inevitably evoke a combination of emotional and rational capabilities and different approaches need to be aligned with situations and contexts depending on the level of complexity at stake and, in some situations, different styles may be adapted before effective decisions are made. Sometimes trade-offs need to be made between strategic and operational targets at multiple functional levels, in order to achieve strategic coherence at the organisational level. To conduct trade-offs in an effective manner, executives need to enhance their strategic agility.

Strategic agility involves being alert to emerging trends, being adept at integrating new possibilities, detaching from past experiences, whilst constantly looking forward and backward at different scenarios, and embracing ideas from all levels of the organisation (top-down and bottom-up) to ensure that optimum value can be generated through limited organisational resources in a dynamic business environment.[21]

Behavioural biases which can be conscious, or instinctive, cognitive or emotional and can be at the individual or group levels, can stifle effective decision-making and limit executives from attaining the critical set of integrated choices required to secure alignment and integration of tactical, operational and strategic objectives. For instance, executives subject to anchoring bias will have the tendency to rely too heavily on the first piece of information offered. Others influenced by confirmatory bias can make conclusions based on preconceived or pre-existing beliefs, experiences and information and dis-confirmatory bias can result in ignoring evidence that runs contrary to expected conclusions. Finally, executives can also suffer from adjustment bias where insufficient adjustments to initial estimates are made, resulting in ineffective decision-making. Failing to address the influences of biases can result in prolongation of decision-making as executives engage in exploring ideas and debating positions, before converging at an optimum outcome.

Decision-making effectiveness also includes consideration of swift action based on incomplete information as waiting for all the information before deciding risks losing valuable momentum. An ex-CEO of Xerox describes the risk of falling into the decision delay trap as follows: 'we really got back into the acquisition market, even though we knew we needed to acquire some things rather than develop them internally. But we got very conservative, very risk averse, and also too data driven. By the time we would reach a decision that some technology was going to be a home run, it had either already been bought or was so expensive we couldn't afford it'.[22]

Conversely, executives should be adept at exiting from bad decisions before these impact on value creation. For example, GE's strategy of building data centres to house the 'Predix Cloud' system was changed swiftly once executives became aware that Amazon.com Inc and Microsoft Corp had invested heavily on data centres for their cloud services, AWS and Azure and GE could not compete with these two in developing cloud technology.[23]

Anchoring of value creation is another important behaviour executives need to exhibit to ensure that all possible scenarios are tested and validated for risks to existing operations and any future growth trajectories.

Decision-makers at the executive level also need to prioritise, process and extract information from various data sources and then combine the relevant information with intuition to determine the best course of action required to address organisational challenges.

Formal review of decision effectiveness can provide important learning points for both seasoned and emerging executives and can serve as resilience test and assessment to determine the suitability of acquisitions, expansion into certain markets, and withdrawal of declining products and services from certain markets. Where relevant past information is not available, then competitor or any comparable cases will be useful to test the resilience of decision effectiveness. Executives can also use scenarios and models developed to test future events to navigate decisions related to unchartered waters such as planning digital disruptions and innovation in new markets.

The combination of default thinking styles, cognitive biases, limited attention spans, information overload, overreliance on past successes, and underestimation of disruptive competitors will drive executives to make wrong or ineffective decisions.

Therefore, decision-making effectiveness at the executive level should account for the following:

a) Value anchoring to ensure that decisions are based on anticipated or measured value instead of other irrational drivers.
b) Bias elimination to secure congruence of tactical, operational and strategic objectives.
c) Distinguishing between trivial and vital data and accurate application of data for accelerated decision-making.
d) Effective combination of relevant information with intuition to generate the best decision outcomes.
e) Acting swiftly to avoid missing out to competitors on strategic opportunities or to avoid significant disruption from new entrants.
f) Decision resilience testing by integration key learning from past events, competitor cases or comparable cases from other sectors.

Some development interventions that executives can deploy to sharpen decision effectiveness in bias elimination include reverse mentoring to address any preconceptions about emerging trends and future scenarios, coaching to challenge group-think and to broaden perspectives on all fronts, and engaging in more formal/structured learning approaches to become more alert to systematic cognitive biases and traps that operate on individuals and groups and to learn how to overcome them. Executives can also use simulations to learn how to deal with complex decision with limited data and time to build on the capacity to act swiftly, validate value anchors and apply intuition to various scenarios. Simulations and action learning projects are also very useful for gaining hands-on experience on modelling strategic objectives and value trade-offs, as well as uncertainties and risks. Executives in matured sectors can also enhance their speed of decision-making by engaging with start-up entrepreneurs thorough reverse mentoring, partnerships or through strategic acquisitions where start-ups maintain their autonomy to challenge executives in the parent organisation to accelerate decision-making. It should be noted that these interventions e.g. simulations and action learning will be covered in more detail in the next chapter.

Future-centric capabilities

Market insight: Executives need to look beyond current context as a means of improving customer experience but also use this as a means of developing the capacity to create disruptive product and services to serve new markets. Enhancing the customer insight capability requires executives to also bridge the gap between customer and organisational expectations where value can be leveraged to provide compelling value propositions across markets. This involves leveraging data and analytics to build a smarter business to better serve customers through more personalised experiences.

Several avenues are open for deepening executive marketing insight such as reverse mentoring within and outside the organisation, participation in ecosystems to understand emerging trends, competitor analysis to gauge the speed and direction of digital disruptions, and strategic review of start-up businesses to determine potential disruptive threats. This can also include understanding the shifts in cultural, value-based systems and demographic changes which will drive customer expectation, experience and emotions to gravitate towards specific products and services. For example, the change in urban customer attitudes towards public transportation has given rise to platform-based companies such as Uber and Lyft to offer services which existing transportation firms were unable to predict. Other platform companies such as Just Eat, Deliveroo Hero AG, Foodpanda GmbH and Grubhub Inc, have also tapped into the gravitation of urban customer behaviour towards takeaway food delivery. Market insight will provide executives with the impetus, drive and confidence to change existing models and to innovate for future customer requirements.

Future orientation: Preparing for the challenges of technological convergence and demographic changes in the workforce includes preparing for automation, artificial intelligence and digital disruptions will require executives to develop capabilities in leveraging analytics, deep learning, social media and intelligent research to position their organisation to launch disruptive models or defend themselves against possible disruptors.

In response to shifting consumer preferences, executives at PepsiCo Inc. have developed a future-oriented business approach by focusing on the health and wellness offerings as one of the company's biggest growth opportunities in order to transform the company to a point where sales growth of healthy products will outstrip the rest of its portfolio.[24]

Future orientation includes developing the capacity to initiate and implement strategies in order to benefit from automation, artificial intelligence and digital disruptions. Given the rapid accelerations experienced in the digital space, it is crucial that executives continue to acquire new capabilities into the effective application of data analytics and insights from artificial intelligence to radically transform business models, enhance customer experience, optimise revenue streams and instigate creative decisions which can enhance organisational value. This will also require executives to develop the right capabilities to navigate the complexity of digital business models, including how to achieve alignment across the dimensions of culture, values, structure, and tasks, and facing the challenges of a constantly evolving digital landscape.

To prepare their executives for future orientation, BASF, UBS and Porsche have joined forces with Mannheim Business School to create a Digital Academy which offers a strategic network for structured exchange of knowledge, experiences, innovations and exploration of future trends by drawing on the expertise of other leading global educational institutions and thought leaders specialising in the evolving digital economic landscape.[25]

Executives can also enhance their future orientation capabilities by cultivating and championing an evolving culture that looks at 'next possibilities and frontiers", rather than dwelling on current and past achievements. They must be willing to embrace chaos and uncertainty and experimentation and be quick to change course and adapt when strategic initiatives fail to yield intended results. They must also pursue initiatives, often based on intuition, using imagination to generate solutions to business challenges.[26] Coaching interventions that focus on cognitive behaviour can be employed to harness the future orientation capabilities of executives at all levels to enable them to drive organsaitional success.[27]

Similarly, it is important for executives to enhance capabilities required to champion and drive efficient delivery of innovation and change initiatives especially in terms of creating and embedding an organisational culture suitable for digital transformation and also to ensure that investment is not wasted on initiatives which fail to deliver intended benefits. Executives will need the right capabilities to deal with transition from old to new business models, legacy infrastructure, and training and development across the entire organisation. These capabilities need to penetrate all levels of the executive team and extend to the operational level leaders to ensure that the digital culture can be enacted and aligned to the organisational strategy and business model.

Because of these shifts to the digital business models, organisations need executives with the right cluster of capabilities to lead teams and partner with the broader ecosystems (includes contractors, the contingent workforce, and crowd talent), make decisions with limited information, think divergently in constructing solutions, and be adaptable, demonstrating resilience in the constantly shifting environment as they lead and drive change. Executives will also need to build resilience in their cognitive, behavioural and emotional intelligence to build and lead teams; keeping people connected and engaged; and driving a culture of innovation, learning and continuous improvement.[28]

IBM, Xerox Nestlé and GE, are amongst the organisations who are developing the capabilities of their top leaders to engage better with ecosystems through various development interventions involving collaborative design, customer experience mapping and problem-solving exercises, to challenge the understanding of how different business functions, industries, and technologies interact, all of which are targeted at enhancing customer experience and to launch innovative products. This suggests that days when leaders reach executive level position based on experience in a sole function have perhaps come to an end.

People-centric capabilities

Ethical capabilities: Ethical capability is another important feature which is often neglected in executive development programmes, but this is crucial for generating long-term growth given that the mismanagement of ethical issues has often resulted in negative outcomes for organisational growth. Ethical capabilities are also linked to embedding a sense of high integrity within all business activities and processes. Lack of ethical intelligence by executives, for instance, is a contributory factor for the PPI fiasco in the UK banking sector where the focus was to generate profits at all cost but then resulted in billions of pounds of fines and huge profits losses. VW's emission fiasco is another example where lack of ethical capabilities resulted in loss of revenue and fines to a firm. The fact that executives and employees in global organisations such as Siemens, Airbus and Rio Tinto have been embroiled in some form of unethical behaviour resulting in financial penalties underscores the challenge that executives face in this area and therefore need regular examination and reviews on this topic.

As organisations seek to deepen customer experience, personalisation and engagement levels, another strand of ethics which executives need to manage effectively relates to means of data acquisition and processes, especially with the promulgation of the GDPR in Europe, which has far-reaching implications for global organisations operating outside this region. This should be carried out with no recourse to inappropriateness nor unnecessary intrusiveness. Thus, executives need to develop the right capabilities that will enable them to drive and embed the right ethical perspective and mindset at all levels of the organisation in terms of compliance and understanding new legislation related to the customer data acquisition, processing and utilisation to develop products and services that are mutually beneficial to customers and the organisation.

Through effective dialogue with stakeholders, executives can gain insight into cultural sensitivities, which can be used to develop unified ethical models which can then be applied to different markets, context and cultures. In addition, executives need to build capabilities to embed these models in the decision-making processes to prevent employees from engaging in unethical practices likely to tarnish the organisational reputation and brand.[29]

Developing ethical capabilities will become more crucial as organisations gain access to customer data and process this information without encroaching on privacy will become more challenging. In addition, developing ethical capabilities and integrity will become more crucial as competition intensifies across all sectors. This will require executives to more frequently make judgment calls on how they can integrate ethical perspectives in developing new disruptive business models and ensure that ethical principles are lived and breathed within the entire organisation and, more importantly, how this ethos can be extended to ecosystem partners.

Building an organisational culture that embraces professionalism and diversity, and that celebrates the uniqueness of individuals is crucial for driving innovation and creativity as this environment expands the scope for smarter ideation and decision-making and limits the risk of silo mentality. Embedding an inclusive culture can broaden the injection of new perspectives that can lead to unearthing previously unrecognised opportunities in products, services, and markets and can be a source for discovering disruptive business models.

To spread the diversity mindset across a wider spectrum of leaders below the C-suite level, Coca cola has established a multicultural leadership council charged with supporting changes in mindsets, behaviours and systems to improve the advancement of multicultural employees. The council's activities include championing the Multicultural Edge – a week-long leadership development programme for building the business acumen of emerging leaders and a year-long leadership development programme designed to strengthen Coca-Cola's pipeline of diverse leaders – and building the Top 10 Multicultural Market Scorecard, which identifies the top ten US multicultural markets and corresponding critical business opportunities for the organisation.[30]

It has also been suggested that organisations with higher proportions of ethnic diversity are more likely to generate better performance compared to competitors as such organisations operate in an environment where diffusion of ideas from different sources is encouraged, non-value adding norms are challenged and there is less propensity to veer towards group think and biases which can stifle innovation and creativity.[31]

The case for inclusive cultures within organisations is becoming more compelling owing to the increasing diversity of talents propelled by demographic changes in the workplace, diversity of markets in terms of shifts towards emerging markets, and diversity of customer choice which is gravitating towards more personalised experiences. As part of creating an enabling environment for employees to experiment with new ideas to serve diverse customer, it is important for executives to instil a prevailing organisational mindset where individuals or groups' unique characteristics are valued and stereotyping is removed at all levels so that unrepresented talent can be tapped to expand the spectrum of ideation that is needed to serve a heterogenous customer and market base.

An inclusive culture can be considered to be optimised if all employees are given the even playing field to contribute to the success without any prejudices and the organisation in turn has systems in place for the recognition of contributions, including appropriate remuneration and rewards.

Some of the avenues executives can deploy to enhance their inclusiveness capabilities include engaging in unconsciousness bias training, reverse mentoring and coaching development interventions to identify and challenge any behaviour patterns that can stifle inclusiveness at the individual/team levels, including how this approach can be measured, monitored, and embedded across the organisation. Effective diversity and inclusion training should address any entrenched unconscious and conscious bias positions, and cover other important areas such as advance communication skills, cross-cultural intelligence, relationship building, and emotional intelligence so that participants can establish commonalities and appreciate the value of individuals from different backgrounds, cultures and ethnicities.[32]

Executives in Nvidia, Rio Tinto and PepsiCo engage in unconsciousness bias training to drive inclusiveness mindset across the executive cohort to enable them transfer this across the leadership chain to set the right climate across the organisations to ensure that under-represented employees can contribute towards organisational goals and open up opportunities at all levels so that a more inclusive, bias-free work environment can be cultivated.

Executives who address unconscious bias and embrace inclusive behaviours will be well positioned to drive value in many fronts. Such executives can adapt their approaches to negotiations to align with the different cultures and geographic locations and to make appropriate decisions tailored to sociocultural environments[33].

Striking the right balance

In mapping out the value-creating executive development capabilities, it is important to strike a balance among the people orientation, results orientation (short and medium) and future centricity (sustainable value and growth) depending on the age, sector and competitor dynamics of the organisation. Organisations that focus only on the present targets are likely to miss out on future opportunities, whereas dwelling entirely on the future can be counterproductive as it will limit the capacity to meet current customer needs which is what generates the capital required to drive investments in future innovations. In organisations operating in mature segments where profit margins are thin and competition is intense, executives can deploy their future-centric capabilities to position the organisations to diffuse any disruptions from startups and develop strong collaborations with other organisations to diversify their portfolio, whilst as the same time becoming more adept at retaining the top 20 percent customer base crucial for generating the cash flow for developing new business models to enhance growth and long-term profitability.

It is important to note that the capabilities listed in table 2 are not sacrosanct and therefore organisations need to account for factors like growth stage of the organisation, sector dynamics and industry-specific capabilities required to drive value. For instance, organisations in the petrochemical and mining sectors must include safety and environmental awareness in the matrix because ignoring these can lead to significant erosion of value, as exemplified by the BP oil spill which attracted a fine of US$13 billion.[34] Also, financial services and utilities sector firms will need to consider any regulatory capabilities required to operate in their respective industries. Similarly, organisations with a global footprint will need to consider capabilities related to managing in the geopolitical, international and cultural environment where their operations are situated as these can have a far-reaching impact on the ability to generate sustainable growth.

Finally, to ensure effective accountability and alignment with the talent development process, it is prudent for organisations to integrate capability profiles of the executive team members (including leaders three tiers below the top) into corporate dashboards that can be monitored at the board level to ensure alignment with strategy and succession planning. Several organisations, including Statoil, BP, Unilever, Johnson & Johnson, Procter & Gamble, GE and Dell have a strong focus on monitoring and reviewing executive capabilities at the board level. This ensures that executive capabilities can be assessed on a regular basis, at the right level within the organisations to determine when new capabilities are required to drive new business models and organisational strategy. This will be explored further in Chapter 4.

Summary of key points

Executives of organisations that are successful at delivering consistent growth through both acquisition and organic routes rely on a wide range of capabilities which are summarised as follows:

Customer impact – Involves managing customer acquisition, retention and lifetime value.

Results orientation – Driving higher performance across business units and operations.

Change leadership – Championing and driving efficient delivery of innovation and change initiatives.

Strategic orientation – Encompasses effective implementation of strategy and clear definition of strategy into tangible steps across business units/divisions.

Business model maximisation – Covers creating and capturing value by rethinking value propositions, identifying unmet customer needs and re-structuring business models.

Mergers and acquisitions insight – Concern strategic acquisitions and mergers to generate value and growth.

External networking capabilities – Deals with effective networking outside the organisation to spot trends and opportunities to drive internal organisational growth.

Decision-making – Entails making effective decisions to seize opportunities to drive value and growth.

Future orientation – Centres on preparing for the challenges of technological convergence and demographic changes in the workforce; includes preparing for automation, artificial intelligence and digital disruptions.

Predicting future customer needs – Covers predicting customer needs through analytics, deep and machine learning, social media and intelligent research.

Market insight – Involves looking beyond current context to provide a compelling offering to meet current customer needs better than competitors.

Team leadership – Deals with the cross-functional collaboration and influence required to drive innovation and problem solving.

Ethical and emotional intelligence – Entails reflection on behaviours, as well as, demonstrating and promoting ethical conduct and integrity.

Inclusiveness – Centres on building a culture that embraces professionalism and diversity, celebrate the uniqueness of individuals.

These capabilities should be linked to results orientation (to address short-term to medium-term goals), people-orientated to create an enabling environment to unleash maximum productivity from employees and must account for future orientation to prepare the organisation for disruptive innovation and long-term survival.

These capabilities can also be mapped onto specific value drivers such as customer retention, innovation and business model maximisation to provide a means of tracking organisational performance, and to gain the support for executives in terms of making time to engage in development interventions required to enhance organisational performance in specific areas.

The emerging digital economy will require executives to consider the human-machine collaboration, its impact on the workplace and how this can be enhanced to deliver value and long-term growth. Executives will need to identify the systems, processes and roles to automate whilst determining which work needs to be undertaken by employees.

This also means identifying new roles and combining others in order to drive productivity, innovation and customer-centric products and services by leveraging the benefits of artificial intelligence and automation.

It is important to strike a balance between the people orientation, results orientation (short and medium) and future centricity (sustainable value and growth) to fit the unique organisational features and characteristic such as age, sector and competitor behaviours.

Organisations need to integrate the capability profiles of the executive team members (including leaders three tiers below the top) into corporate dashboards to allow effective monitoring at the board level to ensure alignment with strategy and succession planning and talent development processes.

References

1. Asmus Komm, John McPherson, Magnus Graf Lambsdorff, and Stephen P. Kelner, Jr., 'Return on Leadership – Competencies that Generate Growth' (Egon Zehnder International and McKinsey & Company, Inc. 2011) https://www.egonzehnder.com/insight/competencies-that-generate-growth-return-on-leadership (last accessed 20 July 2017).
2. Ian Newcomb, 'Three High Street Retailers Which Mastered the On-line Transition' (*Sanderson* 22 July 2014) https://www.sanderson.com/blog/multi-channel/bid/298172/Three-High-Street-Retailers-Which-Mastered-the-Online-Transition (last accessed 30 September 2017).
3. Hay Group, 'The six global megatrends you must be prepared for' (Hay Group 2016) https://www.haygroup.com/leadership2030/about-the-megatrends.aspx (last accessed 30 September 2017).
4. Legal & General Group Plc (Group Strategy 2016) https://www.legalandgeneralgroup.com/about-us/our-strategy/ (last accessed 22 December 2017).
5. Lisa Lacy, 'AI will change everything – even the C-suite' (The Drum 15 May 2017) <http://www.thedrum.com/news/2017/05/15/ai-will-change-everything-even-the-c-suite (last accessed 20 October 2017).
6. Daniel Faggella, 'Artificial Intelligence in Retail – 10 Present and Future Use Cases' (Tech Emergence 29 March 2018) https://www.techemergence.com/artificial-intelligence-retail/ (last accessed 30 March 2018).
7. Lisa Lacy, 'Toyota uses cognitive ads from Watson to introduce the Prius Prime' (The Drum, 15 June 2017) http://www.thedrum.com/news/2017/06/15/toyota-uses-cognitive-ads-watson-introduce-the-prius-prime (last accessed 1 March 2018).
8. Nick Ismail, '3 ways CMOs can meet the c-suite's digital demands' (Information Age 21 July 2017) <http://www.information-age.com/3-ways-cmos-meet-csuites-digital-demands-123467491 (last accessed 20 October 2017).
9. Scott Brown, 'The Under-the-Radar Cisco Leader That Every Partner Needs to Know' (Cisco 9 October 2017) https://blogs.cisco.com/partner/the-under-the-radar-cisco-leader-that-every-partner-needs-to-know (last accessed 2 January 2017).
10. Voicebox Technologies 'Voicebox Partners with Lexus and Xevo to Make Driving Enjoyable and Safe' (*Voicebox Technologies News*) https://www.voicebox.com/voicebox_news/voicebox-partners-with-lexus-and-xevo-to-make-driving-enjoyable-and-safe/ (last accessed 2 January 2018).
11. Alexandra Brown, 'How Zurich Insurance went from pilot to project with AI, IoT and AR' (*Internet of Business* 13 February 2017) (last accessed 2 January 2018).
12. Ilyse Liffreing, 'Kia is seeing 3 times more conversions through its chatbot than its website' (*Digiday* 21 March 2018) https://digiday.com/marketing/personalization-allows-media-optimization-kia-seeing-3-times-conversions-chatbot-website/ (last accessed 30 March 2018).
13. Frank Capek, 'Empathic delivery and the empowered front line' (*Customer Innovations* 15 March 2012) http://customerinnovations.com/empathic-delivery-and-the-empowered-front-line/ (last accessed 30 March 2018).
14. Alice Tybout and Bobby J. Calder, *Kellogg on Marketing* (Wiley 2010) 52.

15. Laurie J. Mullins, *Management and Organisational Behaviour* (Pearson, 2008) 797.
16. Jen Kelchner, 'Sparking change with less pain: An open approach – Digital transformation demands a new approach to change management. Openness provides it' (*Opensource* 3 August 2017) https://opensource.com/open-organization/17/8/digital-transformation-people-2 (last accessed 20 October 2017).
17. Eamonn Kelly, 'The C-suite: Time for version 3.0? Business Trends 2014' (Deloitte Insights, 31 March 2014) https://www2.deloitte.com/insights/us/en/focus/business-trends/2014/c-suite-3-0.html (last accessed 22 October 2017).
18. Elena Lytkina Botelho, Kim Rosenkoetter Powell, Stephen Kincaid and Dina Wang, 'What Sets Successful CEOs Apart' (*Harvard Business Review* May–June 2017) https://hbr.org/2017/05/what-sets-successful-ceos-apart (last accessed 21 October 2017).
19. Jeanne Moore, 'Data visualisation in support of executive decision-making' (2017) 12 *Interdisciplinary Journal of Information, Knowledge and Management* 126.
20. Arun Kumar and N. Meenakshi, *Organizational Behaviour: A Modern Approach* (Vikas Publishing House 2009) 295–96.
21. Marianne W. Lewis, Constantine Andriopoulos and Wendy K. Smith, 'Paradoxical Leadership to Enable Strategic Agility' (2014) 56(3) *California Management Review* 58.
22. Martin Sorrell and Anne Mulcahy, 'How we do it: Three executives reflect on strategic decision-making' (*McKinsey Quarterly* March 2010) https://www.mckinsey.com/business-functions/strategy-and-corporate-finance/our-insights/how-we-do-it-three-executives-reflect-on-strategic-decision-making (last accessed 21 October 2017).
23. Alwyn Scott, 'GE shifts strategy, financial targets for digital business after missteps' (*Reuters* 28 October 2017) https://www.reuters.com/article/us-ge-digital-outlook-insight/ge-shifts-strategy-financial-targets-for-digital-business-after-missteps-idUSKCN1B80CB (last accessed 10 November 2017).
24. John Simons, 'CEOs Should Focus on Long Term, Study Says' (*WSJ*, 27 December 2016) https://www.wsj.com/articles/ceos-should-focus-on-long-term-study-says-1482847202 (last accessed 10 November 2017).
25. Digital Academy, https://www.thedigitalacademy.de/ (last accessed 8 August 2018).
26. Darren Good, 'Cognitive behavioral executive coaching: A structure for increasing flexibility' (2010) 42 *Organization Development Practitioner* 18.
27. John Elkington, 'Boosting Our Future Quotient' (2012) *The Dovenschmidt Quarterly* 34.
28. Anthony Abbatiello, Marjorie Knight, Stacey Philpot and Indranil Roy, 'Leadership disrupted: Pushing the boundaries' (*Deloitte Insight* 28 February 2017) https://dupress.deloitte.com/dup-us-en/focus/human-capital-trends/2017/developing-digital-leaders.html (last accessed 20 September 2017).
29. Vipin Gupta, Transformative Organizations: A Global Perspective (Sage 2004).
30. Coca-Cola Company, 'Diversity Councils and Business Resource Groups' (Coca-Cola Company 2017) (last accessed 27 October 2017).
31. Vivian Hunt, Dennis Layton and Sara Prince, 'Why diversity matters' (McKinsey & Company January 2015) https://www.mckinsey.com/business-functions/organization/our-insights/why-diversity-matters (last accessed 27 October 2017).

32. Kellye Whitney, 'Can you teach diversity and inclusion?' (Chief Learning Officer, 16 May 2017) http://www.clomedia.com/2017/05/16/can-teach-diversity-inclusion/ (last accessed 27 October 2017).

33. Laurence Monnery, Edwin Smelt and Catherine Zhu, 'Great Expectations – How the cultural shift toward deeper diversity can succeed' (*Egonzehnder* 1 January 2017) https://www.egonzehnder.com/insight/great-expectations-how-the-cultural-shift-toward-deeper-diversity-can-succeed (last accessed 20 January 2018).

34. BP Plc (Annual Report 2014) https://www.bp.com/content/dam/bp-country/de_de/PDFs/brochures/BP_Annual_Report_and_Form_20F_2014.pdf (last accessed 27 October 2017).

Building a value-centred executive development architecture

Now that we have identified the capabilities that drive value and growth we can feed them into a robust Executive Development architecture. This architecture or framework needs to account for two overarching factors. First, the executive development architecture must account for both 'soft' and 'hard' dimensions to enable organisations to maximise the benefits of investing in executive development programmes. Secondly, the architecture should be designed and implemented to accommodate the unique characteristics of executive work. Importantly, it should address the constraints limiting executives' ability to develop, transfer and apply the set of capabilities to drive value-creating change projects in organisations. Failure to address the unique characteristics of executives limits the capacity for executives/transfer the learning gained from development programmes to drive organisational value and growth. Three key constraints that executives face relate to their small size relative to other employee cohorts, busy schedules and short tenure. These factors must be considered in designing executive development value-driving architecture. The value-centric executive development architecture/framework is summarised in figure 3.1.

Size: Executives are likely to experience some degree of 'isolation' owing to their relatively small number compared to other employee cohorts; therefore, the 'human capital' executives acquire through development interventions can remain constrained at the top of the organisation unless a suitable means allows transmission of the human capital to drive an enabling environment and motivate employees to create innovative products and services aligned to customer needs. Executives' size constraints can also result in entrenched polarisation and biases which can be embedded within the top team, extend to their immediate direct reports and impede the effective deployment of value and growth capabilities from the top of the organisation to drive the organisation forward. Therefore, executive development programmes should be designed and implemented considering size constraints and incorporate concrete actions and steps to enable participants to remove any biases at the individual and team level; these programmes should also be designed to remove any embedded 'group think'. This will be discussed briefly in the current chapter but more details will be covered in Chapter 4. Consideration should also be given to enhancing the networking capabilities of executives to facilitate leader-leader exchanges as well as leader-team exchanges and reverse mentoring will be useful at enhancing intergenerational talent management.

This approach will deepen the engagement levels across the leadership chain and allow diffusion of knowledge upwards and downwards within the organisation to generate a positive effect on organisational productivity and profitability. The approach will require the executive development span to be extended below the first two tiers below the CEO to allow infusion of different perspectives and challenges to any entrenched biases that may exist within the top executive team. IBM, ABB, 3M and Coca Cola offer executive development to leaders three tiers below the CEO to formulate value-adding solutions from a wider cadre of executives and to boost the talent pipeline for future growth.

Busy schedule: Executives by their nature have extremely busy schedules, packed with meetings, travel, investor briefings, stakeholder and community engagements and this is exacerbated by the vast amount of information they deal with on a daily basis. As a result, executives may consider development programmes as a low priority unless a clear link to value and growth drivers is identified upfront. Even after participating in development programmes, executives' busy schedules imply that opportunities to apply any new capabilities to drive value and growth can be lost to emerging priority issues. The information overload which executives encounter on a daily basis can potentially affect their absorptive capacity, learning preferences and capacity to apply new knowledge effectively to drive the value-centric initiatives and innovation required to generate value and long-term growth. Greater integration of executive development into the workplace activities, provision of multiple learning platforms (such as mobile learning technologies) and bite-size learning, which allows for just-in-time learning, will help minimise the effects of information overload by diluting the benefits of executive development programmes.

Short tenure: The average tenure of most executives ranges between three and seven years with CEOs in FTSE and Fortune 100 companies staying much longer than other C-suite executives such as chief financial officers (CFOs) and chief marketing officers (CMOs), who tend to remain for five years and two years, respectively. This shorter tenure often clashes with the need for executives to balance their own development needs with the pressure of delivering on short-term growth challenges. The unavoidable shorter executive turnover cycle often results in loss of human capital. The effects of this attrition can be minimised by ensuring that the executive development architecture provides for rapid knowledge transfer within the organisation by utilising technology and aligned organisational structures and at the same time allows retention of knowledge within the executive team and the top three leadership tiers to continue any value-centric initiatives after the departure of key executives.

Soft and hard factors

Organisations also need to design and implement executive development architecture which incorporates a wide range of factors, including individual and team dynamics, scalability, sector dynamics, absorptive capacity, transferability, measurability, mode of delivery, content and delivery platforms. These factors can be split into soft (individual and team dynamics and absorptive capacity) and hard (measurability, transferability, context, sector and scalability dynamics, content and delivery platform). Developing and embedding value-centric executive development architecture is crucial as it will guarantee that development programmes drive organisational value and growth and are aligned with the individual executive, team and wider organisational goals.

Executives (individually and collectively) will be better motivated to engage in development programmes and deploy new capabilities to drive organisational value and growth if there is clear articulation of the What's in it for me 'WIF' dimensions. The WIF elements are connected with tangibles such as increased remuneration for effective learning application and non-tangibles such as moving up the talent grid or enhanced promotional prospects. However, linking promotion to participation in executive development can dilute the talent base and unduly increases expectations and should be used sparingly.

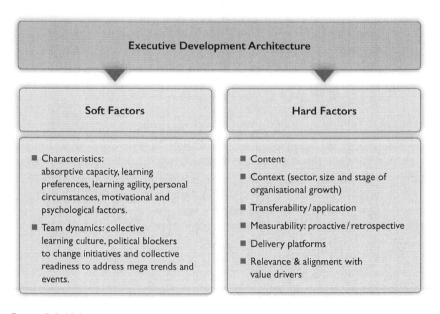

Figure 3.1 Value-centric executive development architecture/framework.

Another important factor which should be considered is the mapping out of preferred learning styles, learning agility, personal circumstances and motivational and psychological factors that will enhance learning acquisition, transfer and application of executive development programmes. Individually and collectively, executives' gaps in addressing business challenges need to be identified and suitable development opportunities should be provided to address this deficiency.

Executives must not underestimate political challenges that can be mounted by peers to derail potential value-centric and growth initiatives. Consideration should be given to enhancing executives' capacity to anticipate and navigate potential political complexities and to win over internal senior stakeholders, as well as external stakeholders like politicians and community leaders internal in the course of managing value-centric initiatives. This is particularly important in the mining sector where governmental and local community interventions are becoming more demanding and affecting the value creation capacity of operations (this is discussed into detail in Chapter 4). Provision should also be made for executive teams to participate in developmental interventions that can drive a 'collective identity' which does not result in 'group think' behaviours that can stifle innovation and growth. Alignment of both the individual and team development must be tracked to assess capacity and readiness to address megatrends and events which can affect organisational value creation and growth. This alignment needs to be assessed, fine-tuned and realigned with the attrition on a continuous basis and, more especially, when there is a major reshuffle within the executive team to maintain the capacity for the organisation to generate value and growth through strategic initiatives.

Absorptive capacity

To counteract the effects of information overload that executives encounter on a regular basis, development interventions must be designed in a manner that is relevant to the current and future business challenges faced by executives, provided in bite size with quick take-away points and linked to immediate challenges. This will increase the assimilation levels of executives engaging in development interventions as there will always be emerging issues from work which shift their attention and priority away from applying new capabilities to driving value and growth.

Content

The content of executive development programmes must align with the achievement of specific strategic drivers such as business model innovation, delivery of cost cutting and M&As. Providing visibility for how the development programmes affect bottom-line performance can stimulate executives' engagement levels as they can visualise the direct and indirect effects of their development on long-term growth of the organisation. To provide executives with a rounded and balanced capability profile, some generic areas need to be included in the design of executive development programmes, including those discussed below.

Developing self-mastery: In terms of effective communication (with regard to developing the gravitas and capacity to influence peers), problem solving, effective decision-making and emotional intelligence to better engage with an ever-increasing span of ecosystem partners are necessary for creating and sustaining disruptive innovative business models and offerings.

Strategic agility and business acumen: developing big-picture thinking, predicting client and stakeholder needs and developing insight into mega events and helping to create disruptive business models and long-term value and growth.

Managing and shaping key stakeholder relations: This involves shaping the key relationships that drive organisational success, including managing board relationships, dealing with the external industry partners and key customers, supply chain and shareholders and managing auditors and regulators.

Blended learning: It is important not to apply the conventional blended development model ratio of 70:20:10 (learning from experience, learning from others and formal learning) carte blanche in designing the content of executive developing content. Formal learning occurs in various forms and includes instructed lead classroom-based sessions, web-based sessions, e-learning courses, curated content on learning management systems (LMS), workshops, seminars and webinars on specialist or generic subjects and has relevance in shaping executives' capabilities, in terms of decision-making, concepts of strategy and effective communication. Informal or experience-based learning which tend to be situated within the workplace and are usually unstructured, encompass a range of modalities such as business simulations, networking, stretch projects, attending conferences, reflection on behaviours and decision-making effectiveness and job rotations (horizontally, lateral and vertical), as well as working within an ecosystem environment, all of which tends to be critical for broadening the capabilities of executives. These approaches are often supplemented by coaching and reverse mentoring to accelerate the effective implementation of learning to drive organisational goals. Other modalities of informal learning can include discussion forums, collaborative platforms, community of practices, and reflective practices. Consideration should be given to the levels of seniority of executives to ensure that the right blend is formulated to meet the development needs and also to ensure better engagement and buy-in from individual executives. For instance, more senior executives will likely follow an 80:15:5 development model if they have already engaged in academic development but need to deepen their experience and exposure in mergers and acquisitions capabilities by learning from their peers (in other divisions or geographic areas) or by engaging in team-based mergers and acquisitions business simulations involving executive peers (from other sectors) to broaden their perspectives on decision-making and to eliminate any potential group-think mentality that may exist within the executive cohort in relation to the business combination and partnering processes. On the other hand, a mid-level executive may follow a 60:20:20 model to consolidate business concepts, develop stronger network across the organisation and build experience in a new business unit. Mid-level executives who want to experience an immersive blended learning environment can explore academic routes. For example, a unique executive programme run by Emlyon Business School employs 'action learning' to build experience of participants to prepare them to launch and commercialise innovative projects in their organisations. The Emlyon programme departs from the traditional educational learning methods, which concentrate on acquiring formal knowledge, and focuses rather on action learning, and prioritising experience where the learner faces a real situation which acts as a catalyst for development, taking them outside their comfort zones and provides participants the platform to learn through experience and remain motivated as this evokes relevance of the learning process and offers better transferability to the workplace. Emlyon's 'Innovation for Growth' programme provides senior executives from large businesses with the platform to experience the dynamic innovative environment of a 'tech' start-up. The programme which is based on four principles: Decentring, Action, Reflexivity and Collaborative Work, runs for between 6 and 12 months and caters for groups of between 15 and 25 employees from the same business.[1] Details of the four principles underpinning Emlyon's 'Innovation for Growth' programme are expanded as follows:

Decentring: provides participants an immersive experience by grouping them into 4 or 5 to align with the needs of a tech start-up with the aim of enhancing their innovation capabilities within an environment of limited resources.

Action: participants within each start-up are required to fully implement a project to resolve a business challenge such as developing a prototype, new product introduction, or penetration into new markets.

Reflexivity: participants are offered sessions to reflect over their challenges with peers and faculty members on managerial practice and business development.

Collaborative work: each group is required to develop a collective and robust proposal, which is presented to the start-up management team for implementation at the end of the programme.

All the four components of the programme challenge participants with different perspectives of how to drive innovation with limited resources, within a relatively short timeframe, which they can be applied to bolster value creation for their organisations in terms of successfully launching of new products, developing of prototypes and penetration of new markets in a cost-effective manner.

Another example of the successful implementation of blended learning for emerging executives and leaders is the Xerox Emerging Leaders Program (ELP) which is an intensive five-month programme that blends face-to-face sessions, web-based learning platforms, online assessment, personal executive coaching and internal mentoring aimed at developing a cadres of leaders capable of managing complex challenges and is commenced with a 'virtual' kick-off session using web-based conferencing and continues with a three-day class room based sessions, supplemented by e-modules on emerging business topics; and then a final two-day, face-to-face sessions supported by individual coaching sessions. Thereafter, participants are required to deliver a business project aligned to the strategic objectives of the company (cost reduction, improvement in product and service quality and delivery of enhanced customer service) which involves working with peers from different functional/cultural backgrounds and the results are presented to a panel of senior executives who evaluate the business potential of such initiatives in driving organisational value and growth.[2]

At Boeing, executive development programmes are mostly led by VP level executives and are designed to embed a collaborative mentality and to align with core strategic values. The programme, which takes a blended approach, involves simulations, action learning and discussion of challenges, and sharing of best practices and experiences.[3]

Airbus has several corporate learning centres where executives expand their capabilities through experiential development interventions, addressing business issues, and by connecting with entrepreneurs, academics and though-leaders to change the organisational culture. This provides an 'outsider' perspective on business challenges and helps to embed an innovative 'start-up' mindset to accelerate the digital transformation pursued by the organisation.[4]

Experiential learning: Experiential learning from real-life and on-the-job experiences, tasks and problem solving is crucial and the most important element of executive development. The most effective approaches include stretch projects, special projects, business simulations, mentoring, coaching, reflective diaries and cross-functional projects and problem-solving, which feature prominently in the executive development programmes of leading organisations such as 3M, Shell and P&G. At Amazon Inc, mentorship programmes are offered to encourage pathways operations managers to locate suitable mentors and to forge networks, and regular one-to-one sessions are arranged with line managers and general managers to facilitate their growth in the role.[5]

Experiential learning is the key pillar of Caterpillar's Leadership Excellence in Accountability and Development (LEAD) programme, which is an invitation-only, executive development programme designed specifically to prepare employees with high potential for future executive-level leadership positions. It takes into account critical learning, formal learning, on-the-job experience and coaching and feedback. Caterpillar partnered with Stanford University to develop the flagship element of the LEAD programme, called Digging Deep, which provides leaders an opportunity to travel to diverse markets such as India, China and Brazil to address real-time business challenges and allows participants to experience Caterpillar's global footprint with a focus on growth markets. Previous participants on the (LEAD) cohorts championed a strategic initiative to transform the organisation's approach to sustainability, making it a core value at Caterpillar.[6]

At Johnson and Johnson, action learning involves multi-national/inter-departmental teams working together to resolve real business challenges involving engagement and communication with politicians, current and potential customers, competitors, supply chain, and consultants. This stimulates collaboration, networking, transfer of ideas into new markets, learning from different management styles, cultures and challenging any biases.[7]

To broaden the experience of C-suite and emerging executives, Coca Cola has developed a culturally immersive development programme to prepare participants to navigate a rapidly emerging business landscape and to deepen passion for the beverage maker's culture, values, and brand.[8] The programme requires participants to travel to an undisclosed Coca Cola operation to resolve an existing business challenge which helps to move them outside their 'comfort zones', develop cultural sensitivity to adjust management styles, sharpen market execution speed and nurture the capacity to make fast-pacing strategic decisions to drive value.

Action and experiential learning can be made more effective by ensuring that various interventions are put in place during the development process and after the event with follow up sessions two weeks, three months and one to two years post event, as detailed below:

During development – Create learning application logs detailing how experiences will be applied to change behaviours (self/team/organisational), address business challenges or initiate disruptive innovation models.

Wrap-up meeting – Team evaluation to identify and rank the most valuable ideas which can address current and future business needs.

Two weeks post event – Follow-up teleconference of all participants to assess status of learning application and challenges encountered taking into account the effects of existing and emerging commitments/strategic business priorities and how these can be managed effectively to deliver targeted benefits of the development intervention.

Three months post event – An in-depth follow-up meeting face to face preferably or by conference call to assess progress of implementation and to unravel any emerging blockers.

One to two years post event – Summary of results of implemented ideas and business impact and develop plans to cascade ideas across the organisation.

Learning from others: Owing to their level of seniority, executives are likely to develop most of their capabilities through feedback from peers and from observing and working with role models /coaches. Learning from others at the executive level can be implemented through a number of avenues, including cross-functional networking, learning from industry networking events, 360-degree feedback, learning from customer interaction sessions, learning from competitors, learning from direct reports, learning from other sectors (e.g. public/private exchange programmes) and collaborative learning with suppliers, academia, and thought leaders.

Formal learning: Formal learning in its different forms provides important conceptual foundations for executives in several areas including strategy, innovation, marketing and finance and, indeed, new frontiers such as artificial intelligence and digital leadership but suffers from disconnect with the workplace. Therefore, it is unlikely to help executives achieve anticipated business outcomes unless it is supplemented by work assignments that consolidate new capabilities and transform learning into the experience and practice required to drive value and growth. To address the limitations of formal learning, the content of executive development interventions must reflect a 'just-in-time' approach, rather than 'just-in-case', so that executives can apply the knowledge promptly to real-time organisational issues to drive value and growth. In addition, executive education programmes can be complemented by mentoring and coaching interventions by senior executives and outside industry executives who can offer different perspectives on how to address challenges faced by the organisation using different approaches.

A range of development activities categorised by education, exposure and experience can be considered in developing the content of executive development programmes, as summarised in table 3.1.

Development activities must also be aligned to the different executive levels as a one-size-fits-all approach will be counterproductive and unlikely to address the capability gaps across the different levels of seniority across the executive cohort. For instance, at the top level, executive coaching augmented by other activities, such as serving on external boards, and customised programmes will resonate better than mentoring or shadowing of other executives (especially within the same organisation or division) owing to the perception that these modalities are more often deployed for junior executive cohorts. Although some senior executives may shrink away from engaging in mentoring as a development intervention (the term may have a condescending connotation associated with it), it can be carefully orchestrated and designed to help participants to enhance a number of capabilities.

Peer to peer mentoring can be effectively deployed particularly for senior executives below and at the c-suite level from within or outside the organisation. An innovative peer to peer mentoring model was initiated at Microsoft, whereby a number of new senior executives (recruited specifically for their entrepreneurial and innovative capabilities) were paired with existing executives of the same levels to serves as a sounding board on creative thinking and

Table 3.1 Executive development activities categorised by education, exposure and experience

Education	Exposure	Experience
Internal education led by executives or external facilitators	Executive coaching (facilitated by superiors, peers and external coaching professionals).	Short-term stretch assignments, practice using new competencies in current role.
External education - academic or leadership development training programme	Mentoring - formal / informal.	Experiential or "action" learning (e.g. games, exercises, simulations, role-play, physical activities, case studies).
Informal learning (learning that takes place without a conventional instructor and outside of structured training)	Internal and external network events.	Job rotation - to another major Strategic Business Units/function/ geographic location.
Just-in-time, agile, scalable training programmes (like the BusinessWeek EDGE program)	Exposure to board of directors (e.g. guest at meetings, face time).	International assignments (multi-country and role exposure).
Connected learning— very different than e-learning	Multi-rater feedback to increase self-awareness.	Assignment with community-based groups and charitable organisations.
Social learning – via LinkedIn, Facebook and similar networking sites	Leadership assessment instrument.	Virtual tournaments and annual strategy offsite events, strategy simulations.
• In-market activities that benchmark like and dissimilar best practices of competing and non-competing companies	Regular cross-functional team meetings to encourage cross-functional learning and teamwork.	Custom simulations that include business acumen, culture, leadership and execution through others, all in one.
• Theatre presentations of strategic concepts to a target group	Peer group meetings with leaders from non-competing businesses to share knowledge and best practices.	Garage entrepreneurial projects in conjunction with internal venture-capital board.
Podcast of interviews	Internal leadership meetings facilitated by an outside agency or consultant.	Action learning tied to strategic imperatives.
	Group-based learning with a futurist.	Business simulation competitions, closely customised to the realities of the actual business.

(Continued)

Education	Exposure	Experience
	Talent forecasting.	Community service programmes that take executives out of their comfort zone and encourage volunteerism and teamwork.
	Team leadership development programme with entire team over three-month period.	Assignments that deepen political skills and reflective practice.
	Diversity in executive training topics, course durations, coaching lengths and training methods to ensure executive development uses a holistic approach.	
	Sound boarding— access to a "strategic thought partner" who acts as a sounding board on any issue; the executive uses the information to further his/her thinking.	
	Systematic and scheduled senior executive involvement in driving quality talent development, review and feedback processes.	
	Targeted development for newly hired executives—executive on-boarding.	
	Networking events with speed-dating presentations on activities occurring across other areas of the business for top executives to identify opportunities for collaboration and takeaways to improve operations.	

to help them expand their capabilities by deepening their experimenting, risk taking and innovative capabilities.[9] This can be an expensive approach and may not be suitable for smaller organisations and the pairing processes needs to be undertaken carefully to derive maximum benefits as wrong connection of individuals with incompatible personalities can produce counterproductive outcomes. This approach also has the benefit of helping the new executives to gain speedy cultural integration from the existing cohort and help them to build a strong network/insight into the value system and other cultural norms of the organisation to hit the ground running right from the start.

C-suite members can develop their capabilities through external mentoring from other peers, non-executive board members or from outside their organisation through external networking professional providers specialising in matching executives with other peers. Some of these providers include Menttium, and Oxford Leadership, which can provide effective pairing arrangements (including training for mentors) to ensure that maximum benefits can be gained from such arrangements.[10]

One of the key areas where peer mentoring can be applied is to develop capabilities in emerging technological areas such as AI, automation and machine learning where executives can be paired with peers who have successfully deployed transformational programmes in these fields to gain support to successfully deliver digital transformation required to drive business model innovation to position the organisation for long-term growth.

Compared to coaching, a well-structured peer to peer mentoring at the executive level can offer participants the benefit of relatable personal experiences, decision-making based on specific business or industry contexts, as well as access to other resources such as network, relevant books and impactful educational programmes which will be beneficial to address specific challenges.[11] This approach can be particularly useful where executives want to accelerate the development of capabilities to address sector specific challenges, such as decision-making, addressing cost-cutting (including embedding efficiencies) and mergers and acquisition.

Development programmes for experienced CEO and C-suite level executives can be targeted at sharpening their capacity to manage diverse complex issues concurrently, and to be more agile at prioritising importance and urgency, and these can be deployed through a number of interventions, including coaching by peers or external providers. Some of the interventions suitable for this cohort include deep-dive sessions within various departments, functions, geographic areas of the organisation, visiting clients in different geographic regions, key customer interaction sessions/customers who have taken business elsewhere, external networking sessions with CEOs from different industrial sectors, providing coaching for other executive members (as a means of reflecting on own leadership style and behaviour), cultural and ethical sensitivity training, interactions with leading academics and organisational leaders of disruptive/emerging technologies from unrelated sectors, listening to selected Podcasts, selected reading lists, and engaging in regular

1:1 sessions with retired CEOs in similar industries, merger and acquisition targeting and analysis, decision-making techniques, and reverse mentoring. Other modalities suitable for this cohort include speed-dating sessions with thought leaders and attending and presenting at conferences, summits and events.

Cisco for example offers executives an interactive thought leaders programmes with speakers drawn from multiple countries to share insights on emerging trends across sectors. Following the presentations, executives and the speakers delve into detailed in-depth discussions, including economic analysis and modelling to quantify the business case for any emerging opportunities through video-conferencing facilities.[12]

Executive coaching can be adapted to meet the needs of the individual and to enable them to navigate challenging business issues. It also offers participants the privacy and the opportunity to confront their vulnerabilities, and to engage in reflective thinking to determine the best solution(s) required to address business challenges. Sam Walsh, the former CEO of global mining giant Rio-Tinto validated business ideas with his executive coach, Paul Victor of Vmax, a Doctor of Psychology with a manufacturing background who assisted him, particularly when entering the unchartered territory of restructuring the business whilst maintaining the focus on getting the balance right between present and future perspectives.[13] This exemplifies how executive coaching can be deployed to help CEOs and other senior executives to navigate emerging challenges, make appropriate strategic choices and to position the organisation for future success.

Attending or presenting at conferences (industry or non-industry related) is a useful development modality for C-suite executives and can be an avenue for developing networking capabilities, identifying peer mentors and for gaining early insight to any mega trends or events which can impact on the ability to generate long-term value. There are several conferences such as the AI Expo Europe, Adobe Summit, Corinium Forums, Disruption Summit Europe, European banking Forum, Digital Utilities Europe, The Future of Mining, Digital Strategy Innovation Summit, Startup Grind Europe Conference which are suitable for the C-suite and other levels of executives. Corinium, for example, provides forums across multi-continents, where executives can connect with peers with a successful track record of driving the transformation of the digital economy in data analytics, customer experience, artificial intelligence and other emerging technological advances to transfer learning to transform their own organizations.

This cohort of executives can also benefit from appreciative inquiry training which can inspire new approaches to thinking when enacting business transformations and strategic planning processes.[14] Appreciative Inquiry generally involves identifying and focussing on the positive outcomes rather than the problems encountered by the organisation and can therefore bolster executives' confidence owing to the emphasis on strengths rather than problems. However, care must be taken in following this approach as decision-making based solely on this approach can be unbalanced and can lead to over-confidence as it fails to take into account critical past failures and issues which can provide key learning points for driving future value.

For vice-president (VP) level executives and below, development interventions combining coaching, reverse mentoring, job assignments, networking, customised programmes and trend-spotting can be deployed to address specific gaps in capabilities. One means of implementing trend-spotting as a development initiative is for one person to brief other executives about two or three emerging trends as ice-breakers during weekly and monthly meetings at divisional or department levels. These ideas can be summarised and shared on knowledge hub platforms shared by all executives. Any emerging themes can be checked against current and future strategy for robustness or to identify suitable disruptive projects which can be launched to drive organisational value.

Senior executives including CEOs and VPs at several organisations such as Nestlé, BNY Mellon, Cisco, AXA, JP Morgan Chase, Microsoft, and Xerox are embracing reverse mentoring (an initiative that facilities cross-generational relationships building and learning whereby an older executive is paired with and mentored by younger employee or subject matter expert on topics such as current trends, social media, technology, behaviour patterns and preferences of younger generations). If designed properly, this modality can help to address gaps on both sides (executives versus younger generation) and provide an exchange platform where weaknesses/strengths on both sides can be addressed. Junior colleagues and digital native/astute individuals (external to the organisation) can engage in interactions with executives in order to increase the accurate assessment of younger generation talent/potential, drive the implementation of effective diversity programmes and create an inclusive mindset (by helping executives to understand the perspectives and challenges of a younger generation workforce from different cultural or ethnic backgrounds). Junior staff participating in reverse mentoring can also benefit by accelerating the acquisition of critical leadership skills and build more gravitas and political capabilities through their interactions with senior executives in an informal environment. With younger generation employees now having a greater expectation for executives to exhibit stronger interpersonal skills, underpinned by greater informality, effective communication and emotional intelligence,[15] reverse mentoring will continue to be a critical component of executive development.

Reverse mentoring also helps executives to grasp different avenues to leverage new trends in social media, mobile technology and emerging consumer preferences to strengthen the business's competitive edge.

At BNY Mellon, reverse mentoring has assisted executives, including the CEO, to develop better understanding of how technology is shaping the business, to provide adequate technological tools for employees necessary for addressing emerging challenges and to predict the expectations and needs of future clients to determine how the organisation can adapt to these trends.[16]

Similarly, Microsoft executives employ reverse mentoring to design digital communication to foster intergenerational relations, provide suitable workplace design, explore innovative avenues to engage fully with younger talent via social media optimisation (making maximum use of the various social media channels and tools to engage with a wider audience), and ultimately to gain insight into meeting future customer needs.[17]

Other benefits of reverse mentoring include helping executives to avoid optimism bias by considering challenges from wider perspectives, accelerating innovation culture and injecting fresh perspectives to remove groupthink mentality. Reverse mentoring also enables executives to reflect on their leadership styles, values and ethos and how these resonate throughout the organization.

In addition to reverse mentoring, executives can select peer-level mentors from different sectors to broaden their perspectives on addressing digital transformation and emerging trends.

Customer Experience Initiatives (which involves interactions and discussions with key customers to determine their pain points in the purchasing decision process) can also provide executives in the retail and consumer goods sector with better insight into the entire customer experience journey to understand at first-hand how customers engage in their buying decisions, interact with mobile technology and other omni-channels, and how the organisation can position advertising and price-matching schemes to appeal to tech-savvy customers.

Competitor Analysis can enable executives to embrace a more contingent approach to decision-making, challenge entrenched positions and realign business models to fast-moving competitive landscape as it can provide some insight into the general direction of the industry and any potential under-exploited opportunities that others have failed to identify.

For executives in the lower tier and high-potential bracket, development job assignments, mentoring and executive coaching can be deployed as well as appreciative inquiry training to broaden their capabilities in decision-making and effective communication to break down silos in organisational structures, offer fresh perspectives to challenge the status quo, thereby promoting innovation and collaboration. At Zensar Technologies (an information technology services and infrastructure services provider with headquarters in Pune, India and a customer base spanning 29 global locations) managers at all levels are offered training in appreciative inquiry to engage in constructive conversations to break down silos and resolve business challenges.[18]

The development programmes for high-potential executives should focus on change projects that can shift entrenched paradigms to inculcate deep reflection and drive greater cross-functional collaboration to create impact at the individual, team and organisational level as executives in this cohort are the agents for change and develop the critical mass to generate disruptive business models. To assist high-potentials and even more senior executive cohorts in mastering the practice of reflection in a business context, two separate models developed by Gibbs and Mezirow are combined as depicted in figure 3.2. Six of the steps in Gibbs' reflective cycle are retained and are supplemented by two steps from Merizow's ten-step model (exploration and embedding) to allow executives to develop solutions to issues unearthed during reflection and building new perspectives which are important steps omitted from Gibbs' cycle. Brief descriptions of all the eight steps in the combined reflective cycle is outlined below to assist application to real-life situations.[1]

Description: Review of the event, decision or experience, including the context under which it occurred, possibly with all parties involved, mapping out any patterns of perceptions formed.

Feelings/reaction: What emotional responses were evoked by you and other parties who witnessed the decision or event and what contextual factors influenced your/their feelings, reaction and response.

Evaluation: Consideration of the good and bad experiences, including possible impact on personal and professional values, beliefs and assumptions. Identifying any new capabilities gained from the current experiences and how these resonate with previous experiences or events.

Analysis: Identification of the root causes and how you/others contributed to the event or decision. What factors may constrain you from acting in new ways and how you plan to address them.

Figure 3.2 Reflective cycle based on Gibbs and Mezirow models.

Exploration: Review of new experiences, roles, and relationships required to move to a desired state or in line with organisational/personal values, beliefs or behaviours. What steps can be taken to reinforce positive outcomes and prevent lapsing into negative territory or unacceptable behaviours or actions.

Conclusion: What learning has been gained. How are negative events going to be avoided in future and how can positives be reinforced or improved.

Action Plan: What training, experiences and challenges will be pursued to reinforce positives and avoid negative events.

Embed: Application of new capabilities, building new behaviours and perspectives to consolidate personal and professional practice in line with organisational values and beliefs. Leveraging exemplary behaviours to influence peers, direct reports and others outside direct sphere of control.

The above model can also be applied to team reflective situations and used to support coaching sessions involving both executives and other employees.

Another effective modality for high-potentials is tapping into the expertise of innovative entrepreneurs and leaders of innovation hubs who can serve as 'residence' for some of the organisation's business offerings such as the approached used by GE to enhance the entrepreneurial mindset of its leaders, providing coaching to shift the traditional silo mindset of business leaders in order to launch its digital innovation business model.[19]

Compelling storytelling can also be employed to reinforce learning, prompt swift action, bring facts and figures to life, create emotional connections with organisational values, change attitudes and behaviours, and, importantly, instigate action for high-potential executives.

Accountancy firm KPMG for example launched a company-wide storytelling initiative in order to re-establish its sense of purpose and build a stronger emotional link with staff across the globe. This initiative which was dubbed the 'Higher Purpose' initiative elicited stories from employees at all levels from interns to the Chairman about how their work made a difference and the outcome of this initiate resulted in increased employee engagement and commitment to organisational goals.[20]

For the executive cohort, storytelling can be used to prompt action by exploring various scenarios (win–win, win–lose or lose–lose) about business challenges and opportunities, customer journey narratives and real-time examples of how other peers have addressed challenges including how key takeaways can be employed to address current business challenges. Senior Executives can use stories about their own experience of different merger and acquisition negotiations to highlight the implications of win–win, win–lose or lose–lose scenarios and what potential pitfalls emerging executives can avoid in future. Stories about the in-store journey of customers can also be used to identify customer pain points, questions and concerns, opportunities for cross-selling, which will also provide ideas for creating disruptive product and services and help the organisation to develop relevant omni-channels to deepen customer experience.

Digital tools can also be employed to invoke an immersive story telling experience by combining great imagery and audio effects to create an intense emotional connection to help executives visualise/appreciate the consequences of their action and thereby prompt adjustment in behaviour and help them to drive change in an impactful manner.

Development programmes for organisations with international operations must equip executives to build capabilities related to effectively navigating regional geo-political, local and global issues and managing inclusiveness and meritocracy in diverse cultural environments. Multinational organisations can reduce the cost of developing executives by leveraging technology. For example, organisations like Cisco, Microsoft and ABB deploy webinars and deliver sessions by subject matter experts to build communities of practice/experts across divisions and to drive consistency in approach across countries and to reduce the cost of executive development programmes.

It is also important to evaluate the limitation and benefits of the most popular forms of executive development modalities; coaching, action learning, podcasting, gamification, and virtual/augmented reality (technology that displays or overlays virtual images or views over real world environments). These are detailed in tables 3.2 to 3.7 and allows organisations to determine the most effective modalities to invest in order to close the gaps in specific value driving capabilities. This will also enable the best approaches to be adapted for individual, team and organisational level needs, whilst ensuring that any pitfalls are augmented by other modalities to maximise the return of investment from executive development interventions.

Table 3.2 Executive Coaching: limitations and advantages

Executive Coaching - Exposure

Advantages	Limitations
• The ROI can be easily monitored at the individual / team levels. • The investments can be reasonably lower compared to other interventions such as action learning and executive education. • Can be designed to fit the individual / teams' schedules and can occur within the workplace. • Can offer just-in-time learning with personal accountability for development. • Improves self-awareness, thinking capabilities and opportunities to learn from mistakes. • Provides executives with the confidentiality if external resource is used. • Team/Group coaching can unify the executives to work on a common goal and drive them to achieve performance targets.	• Can prove challenging when this intervention is systemised across executives within a large organisation compared to executive education and other modalities. • Executives can become disengaged due to the lack of continuity / clarity during the coaching sessions / process. • It may be challenging to find a coach with suitable capabilities / expertise to meet the unique individual / team needs.

Table 3.3 Action Learning: limitations and advantages

Action Learning – Experience & exposure

Advantages	Limitations
• Can be beneficial even for the very experienced senior executives. • Can provide substantive ROI in a relatively short timeframe. • Can potentially provide the highest ROI compared to other development interventions. • The locus or onus of success lies with the participants.	• More expensive intervention per participant/day than other development interventions. • Can require extensive time commitments and resources to deliver this modality effectively. • Due to its real-time nature, action learning can sometimes be challenging to cascade across a team or multinational organisation. • Requires effective facilitation and management to transfer learning outputs into organisational outcomes.

Table 3.4 Gamification/Simulation: limitations and advantages

Gamification/Simulation – education and exposure

Advantages	Limitations
• Allows for instantaneous feedback such as leader boards and dashboards. • Can influence the emotional connection with the learning material and promotes retention. • Allows learners to engage with peers and provides significant gains through discussion, idea generation, feedback, and support. • Stimulates collaborative behaviours since it closely emulates the cross-functional exchange of information that transpires in the work environment. • Can help to reinforce the business context through the use of storytelling techniques.	• Designing the content to connect with organisational strategic goals and objectives can be a challenging task. • Initial and ongoing investments can be high and may need further adaptation of content on multiple platforms such as desktop, mobile, and tablet devices.

Table 3.5 Podcasting: limitations and advantages

Podcasting - education

Advantages	Limitations
• Provides a portable and immersive learning experience which can be fitted around the busy schedule of executives	• Time consuming to develop useful content or locate existing podcasts that are relevant to the business needs.
• As a form of digital media, it is easy to measure podcast listenership and popularity.	• Measuring the performance impact can be challenging as the transfer of learning into action cannot be easily tracked compared to other forms of interventions such as action learning.
• Can track the number of downloads of individual episodes as well as subscribership to shows.	

Table 3.6 Virtual/Augmented Reality: limitations and advantages

Virtual/Augmented Reality – exposure and education

Advantages	Limitations
• Inherently perceived as an innovative approach and hence more attractive to millennial executive cohort.	• Higher cost and difficulty in creating content that can address the inherent complexities and challenges experienced by an organisation.
• Provides an immersive learning environment which can improve engagement, retention and recall.	• Suitable for shorter development interventions as overexposure to the technology for longer periods can result in distractions.
• Suitable for different learning styles and can be used to simplify complex problems.	• If poorly designed, participants can become easily disengaged resulting in limited impact on organisational performance.
• Allows real-time multinational team-building / learning activities to be held, reducing the cost of travel.	
• Enables the facilitation of coaching for teams and groups.	
• Improves collaboration and establishes a 'presence' for geographically dispersed executive training.	

Table 3.7 Executive Education: limitations and advantages

Executive Education – education

Advantages	Limitations
• Interventions are normally easier for senior management and HR team to pilot and test before cascading to other teams. • Usually less cost per person/day if intervention runs for a shorter duration. • Easier to design, implement and control compared to other modalities such as action learning. • Can be creatively and properly designed, to target specific individual and/or organization development impact. • This modality is useful for conveying facts, concepts, principles, attitudes and problem-solving skills and can be supplemented by case studies, audio-visuals and discussions.	• Getting Participants to pilot an intervention may be more challenging than other approaches as this may be perceived to be an academic process with no link to business drivers. • Can be perceived as irrelevant academic process if it is poorly designed. • Can be less engaging and result in loss of learning transfer if immediate connection with business needs and value drivers cannot be identified by the executive. • ROI may be difficult to track if the link to business needs are not integrated into the design. • It may be challenging to design this intervention to address individual capability gaps / wider team needs concurrently.

Delivery platform/channels

Some of the objections that executives associate with formal learning activities can be addressed by designing the delivery mechanism to meet the unique needs of the executives (isolation, busy lifestyle and information overload). One possible solution is to combine synchronous with asynchronous learning delivery platforms (see table 3.8) to provide executives with the flexibility and opportunity to interact with peers in their own time and space to discuss pertinent strategic and operational issues. Synchronous platforms also provide a degree of interactivity to minimise the effects of the isolation syndrome that an executive may face by learning alone. It also offers the flexibility to engage in just-in-time learning to suit their busy lifestyles and can be tailored to address their individual needs. For example, BP has launched a programme to develop a number of apps to train business leaders more effectively, dubbed 'SatNav', for leadership. The apps, which are underpinned by BP's high production values, are based on techniques used in computer games and offer high-quality video and interactive modules. The apps are designed to make training for BPs business leaders and managers more effective; they give the executives access to just-in-time information and practice, reduce

Table 3.8 Synchronous and asynchronous learning delivery platforms

Synchronous Learning	Asynchronous Learning
Video / teleconferencing / mobile	Blogs
Web conferencing / webinars	Podcasts
Chat / instant messaging	Simulations
Wikis and virtual collaborative workspaces (Microsoft SharePoint and Google Docs)	Gamification, goal-based scenarios
	Social networking tools - LinkedIn

the time it takes business leaders to become competent in their roles and provide them with support and learning materials at key transition points, including providing anonymised feedback from direct reports on leadership performance.[21]

Combining both approaches (synchronous and asynchronous) allows the customisation of learning and provides executives with an 'authentic' experience for the 10% of the learning which is often covered through face-to-face delivery. Asynchronous learning methods such as simulation, gaming and goal-based scenarios enable executives to experience 'real-world situations' within a safe environment to practice, make mistakes and acquire new capabilities. Simulations can also be tailored towards specific audiences by providing a learning experience that is more hands-on for executives based on their job role and complexities. For example, simulations can enable a utility company to determine optimal pricing, robustness of investment planning, M&A and integration priorities and to experiment with new business models while anticipating and reacting to the actions of competitors, regulators and the possible financial impact under various scenarios. This can enable participants not only to formulate effective strategic responses to possible contingencies, but also to get into the competitor's or regulator's mindset and to make decision based on a wider stakeholder perspective. Simulations can also offer an immersive experience and can challenge executives to grow through reflection and experimentation and take immediate action to address business challenges. They also enable learning across functions, cultures and global markets, and allow participants to appreciate the underlying causes and effects on business operations, departments and functions by unveiling what-ifs and omissions, as executives reflect on their strategic choices during simulation exercises. This modality of development can allow collaborative interactions and also provide the experience of dealing with exogenous shocks (new technologies, economic-political events) which enable participants to develop the skills to stay agile and flexible in the face of changing business situations. The resulting improvement in decision-making capabilities as well as enhanced cognitive capacity can prepare participants to respond to similar events in the real-world scenarios within a relative short time, compared to other forms of development such as reading books or attending corporate education programmes.

Notwithstanding the immediate benefits stated above, simulations can suffer from lack of direct application opportunities and a possible time-lag in learning. This deficiency can be addressed by combining this approach with other development modalities such as action-learning to ensure transfer of learning to address real business issues.[22]

Developing capabilities through reading of selected books is a popular approach, which resonates with many executives including CEOs. The CEO of Dropbox attributes his success and development to frequent reading of business books and has introduced this concept to this executive team events where ideas from new books are discussed[23].

Virtual, augmented and mixed reality technology is transforming the gamification and experiential learning space of executive development by providing an immersive experience which involves being able to create interactive holographic scenarios to address business challenges during development events and offers a unified platform for specialist thought leaders and technical experts to interact with participants, breaking down time and distance barriers. The use of Microsoft HoloLens (a device which is based on augmented reality and permits users to engage with digital content and interact with holograms which can be moved, shaped and pinned or anchoring to provide real world visualisations in three-dimensional environment) for instance is being embedded within AI technology to make real-time predictions and to enhance the decision-making capabilities of executives.[24]

Virtual Reality/Augment Reality headsets equipped with eye-tracking systems will also allow executives to gauge when they are tired and not assimilating information effectively during development sessions.[25] However, the initial investment could be prohibitive for smaller organisations and may require staff who are skilled at monitoring these systems to derive maximum benefits from this technology and will therefore be more suitable for larger organisations and training institutions and providers who can benefit from the economy of scale from procuring large quantities.

An 'app' based augmented reality technology developed by BP with Somo (a mobile and connected solutions company) can be adapted to support virtual action learning (action learning which with participants working from remote locations to address a business challenge) by executives. The multi-touch table (Learning Lens) which allows multiple participants to simultaneously access 360 degrees visualization content of upstream technologies from around the world through the app and makes provision for the inclusion of additional course-specific tutorials, details of challenges encountered from action learning projects and sharing of success stories[26]. This technology has the potential for integration into other modalities of informal learning such as simulations scenarios to enhance the decision-making capabilities of executives working in the same or different geographic locations which may have a large initial cost overlay but the cost benefits can be off-set against travelling cost and assessed in more detail during the ROI stage which is discussed in Chapter 7.

Context

Sector dynamics: There are specific sectors insights and dynamics which executives need to master to generate innovation solutions/disruptive models. In addition to the core capabilities that are common across industries (e.g. managing diversity, engagement), executive development programmes need to be tailored to address industry/sector-specific capabilities required for value creation and long-term growth. This subjected is expanded upon in Chapter 4.

Scalability: Executive development programmes must be scaled to the size of the organisation. Larger organisations often face very complex structures and systems and the scale of challenges they experience far outweighs what their small and medium-sized enterprise (SME) counterparts go through; therefore, size factors need to be built into the design of executive development programmes. Specifically, development programmes for larger organisations must equip executives with insight, leadership and decision-making capabilities to dismantle entrenched cultural and structural factors that can impede learning transfer and behaviour transformation, and engender an enabling environment in which front-line staff embrace the propensity to implement operational changes to drive value and growth. Although large firms suffer fewer resource challenges, they tend to face limitations in transferring learning across widely dispersed executive teams and organisations to drive the needed changes necessary for creating value. Therefore, one of the scalability considerations that large organisations need to build into the architecture of executive development is a structure for knowledge transfer within the executive team and across the organisation. To address these challenges, larger organisations should develop knowledge management platforms (these are discussed in Chapters 6 and 7), where key learning from executive development can be distilled and cascaded across the executive team and wider organisation. This can be augmented by promoting frequent informal executive interactions (such as Drop-ins' sessions with the CEO and the executive teams, Staff briefings, interactive webinar sessions, and active participating in discussions forums or internal communication platforms) to serve as a catalyst for sharing best practice ideas and embed learning. At Swiss Re, best practice opportunities are integrated into the global travel schedules of executives. In any country they visit, the executive has a three-hour knowledge transfer slot to learn new cultural and operational perspectives irrespective of the portfolio of operation/products under their jurisdiction.

Smaller firms usually face resources constraints and hence need to explore low-cost informal development interventions involving; engaging in collaborative activities in areas such as marketing, research and development with larger or smaller industry (in both related and unrelated segments) partners and universities, network-based learning, reading books, reverse mentoring (with executives in larger organisations) and customer interactions/deep dive sessions to build the capacity to provide value-centric services and products necessary for driving growth. Other low-cost avenues smaller firms can explore include asynchronous learning, such as podcasts, blogs and free courses; for example, futurelearn, London School of Business and Finance Global MBA, MIT Sloan School of Management, Kutztown University Online Learning Programs, Free Management Library, Businessballs, HP Learning Center, Managing the Digital Enterprise (www.digitalenterprise. org), The OpenCourseWare Consortium, Coursera, Udemy, edX, Khan Academy, Openculture, offer a range of business-related courses at zero cost. More details about organisational size implications on executive development is discussed in Chapter 4.

Phase in organisational growth: Another important contextual factor needing consideration in developing value-creating executive development programmes is the phase of organisational growth. In the early phase of organisational development, there is a high propensity for the executives to become innovative to disrupt the market with new products and services. At this stage, executive development should be geared towards enhancing executives' capabilities to challenge assumptions to expand innovation to the next frontier whilst balancing this with broader market penetration capabilities (Chapter 1). For more mature organisations, there is less motivation for executives to challenge assumptions and therefore they become more risk averse and less adaptive to customer needs. Hence, executive development for more mature organisations should focus on addressing issues of vision, currency, adaptability, business model innovation and risk tolerance and how these are deployed to drive value and growth. Thus, a value-centric executive development programme at this stage should focus on producing the right balance of capabilities that enable executives to achieve the appropriate level of innovation or adaptability behaviours for this stage of organisational growth. For less matured organisations characterised by inability to maximise existing business opportunities and declining sales, a more engaging and nurturing approach to executive development should be adapted with oversight from the CEO and the board ensuring that executives and leaders up to three levels below the C-suite are actively developing their capabilities, which are tied to performance review and bonuses. The cultural climate for learning amongst the executive cohort can help determine readiness for a shift to a more aggressive level of learning and should be included in the design process of any development programmes to ensure early buy-in from the executive cohort. The design process should also promote better engagement/ commitment from executives by ensuring that the identification/selection of relevant value drivers is led by the executive cohort and not imposed on them by others.

Transferability/Application

Transferability and application of learning must be integrated upfront in the design of value-centric executive development programmes. Transferability and application of learning from executive development programmes to deliver unique solutions, transform organisational structures and shift counterproductive culture, behaviours and value systems is fundamental to driving value and growth. Lack of transfer and application opportunities post-event will trigger rapid decline in new knowledge/capabilities gained by executives and limit/delay the expected return on investment projected from such interventions. The transferability of learning and application of new capabilities should not be limited to a business unit or the immediate span of control of executives; rather, cross-functional or organisation-wide support is required to establish an enabling cultural environment, influence innovation and customer service improvements and drive long-term organisational value. Integrating transferability and application requirements into the executive development programmes from the outset will enable executives to identify and manage expectations and plan data collection requirements effectively. Relegating the application/transfer to the end of the development journey will erode the opportunity to maximise the impact of the development intervention on the value creation and growth process. Owing to the importance of transferability and learning application to value creation and growth, this will be expanded further in Chapter 7.

Measurability

Setting expectations around the intended impact of an executive development programme on specific value and growth drivers must be an integral component of the executive development architecture. These expectations should be translated into both tangible and intangible measures to enable executives and the organisation to support the effective evaluation of the value created through the executive development programmes, without which it will be difficult to secure any further investment in such activities. Early integration of these measures (tangible and intangible) into the executive development architecture and clearly setting out the expected impact of how these programmes will be measured and evaluated are crucial in establishing a credible return on investment (ROI) for such programmes. Leaving the measurement decision to the end of the development process can result in limited or no data capture, whilst integrating the measurement requirements upfront into the executive development architecture will enable executives to plan and prepare to capture records (learning logs, pre/post behaviour audits, 360-degree evaluations, video interviews) during and after the development programme backed by stories of how new capabilities have been applied to drive value and growth. At the Shell Project Leadership Academy, executives and leaders (up to the

VP level) are required to create a log of their experiences and reflections across various capabilities which are then linked to specific value created in terms of business outcomes. This approach of embedding measures at the onset of the development programme enables executives to connect the acquisition and application of new capabilities to specific business outcomes. This connection is reinforced when executive development is included in the performance objectives of executives with indicators related to intangible indicators such as behaviour change, networking capabilities, learning transfer and facilitating the achievement of cross-departmental or multi-departmental goals. These measures can also be expanded to include individual indicators (self-mastery and reflection), team indicators (team cohesion and identity) and organisational indicators (percentage of executives retained post development). According to Nick Shackleton-Jones, director of online and informal learning at BP, 'Building in the measures of performance into the learning itself provides you with a massive stream of data about how leaders are performing day to day, and helps you to see the impact of the learning interventions you introduce'[16].

Building in soft (individual and team dynamics) and hard factors (content and delivery platforms, context (sector, size and stage of organisational growth), transferability/application, measurability) into the executive development architecture will enable organisations to appreciate the significance of developing and embedding value-centric executive development architecture. This will provide further assurance that development programmes are still aligned with the individual executive, team and wider organisational goals and can be leveraged to drive organisational value and growth. Further details on measuring the impact of executive development will be covered in Chapter 7.

Assessment of executive development effectiveness

A high-level assessment of the effectiveness of an executive development programme can be undertaken by plotting the robustness and breadth of the executive development architecture against the degree of connectedness of executive development programmes to value-centric and growth drivers of an organisation (see figure 3.3).

Where there is a less developed/robust executive development architecture' (taking into account both soft (individual and team dynamics) and hard factors (content and delivery platforms, context (sector, size and stage of organisational growth), transferability/application, measurability) coupled with minimal connectedness to growth drivers, an organisation will be considered to be in the emerging phase in terms of the effectiveness of its executive development. Conversely, where evidence suggests broad coverage of the components of the executive development architecture is matched by a very strong connection to value-centric and growth drivers, then an organisation's executive development can be considered to be in a high-performing stage.

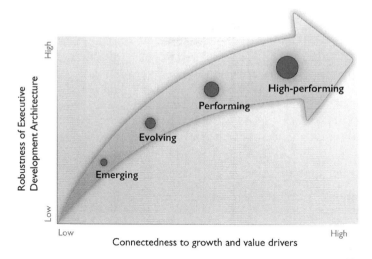

Figure 3.3 Executive development assessment model.

Summary of key points

Three key constraints which prevent learning transfer from executive de-velopment interventions in organisations relate to the small size of the executive cohort, their busy schedules and their short tenure. These fac-tors must be considered in designing executive development value-driving architecture.

Organisations also need to design and implement executive development architecture which incorporates a wide range of factors, including individual and team dynamics, scalability, sector dynamics, absorptive capacity, trans-ferability, measurability, mode of delivery and the content and structure. These factors can be split into soft (individual and team dynamics and ab-sorptive capacity) and hard (measurability, transferability, context, sector and scalability dynamics, content and delivery platform).

Development activities must be aligned to the different executive levels as a one-size-fits-all approach will be counterproductive and unlikely to address the capability gaps across the different levels of seniority across the executive cohort. For instance, at the top level (C-suite), executive coaching augmented by other activities, such as serving on external boards, and customised pro-grammes will resonate with this cohort.

Similarly, experienced CEO and C-suite development programmes can include deep-dive sessions within the organisation, visiting clients in dif-ferent geographic regions, customer interaction sessions, external network-ing sessions with CEOs from different industrial sectors, and coaching from other executive members (as a means of reflecting on own leadership style and behaviour).

The limitations and benefits of the most popular forms of executive development modalities—coaching, action learning, podcasting, gamification, and virtual/augmented reality—need to be considered as this allows organisations to invest in the most effective modalities.

A high-level assessment of the effectiveness of an executive development programme is offered by comparing the robustness of the executive development architecture with the degree of connectedness of executive development programmes to value-centric and growth drivers of an organisation.

Note

1 J. Mezirow, 'Learning to think like an adult: Core concepts of transformation theory' in E. Taylor and P. Cranton (eds), *The Handbook of Transformative Learning: Theory, Research, and Practice* (Jossey-Bass 2012) 73–96.

References

1. Centre for Creative Leadership, 'Blended learning prepares leaders around the world' (Centre for Creative Leadership March 2015) http://www.ccl.org/wp-content/uploads/2015/03/Xerox_Corporation.pdf (last assessed 30 November 2016).
2. EmLyon Business School, Innovation for Growth Programme: Experience start-up innovation (EmLyon Business School) https://executive.em-lyon.com/en/Corporate-solutions/Develop-your-employees-skills/Learning-through-action/Innovation-For-Growth (last accessed 20 November 2016).
3. Frank Kalman, 'Corporate Spotlight: Boeing's Leadership Center' (Chief Learning Officer, 1 February 2012) http://www.clomedia.com/2012/02/01/corporate-spotlight-boeings-leadership-center/ (last accessed 16 June 2017).
4. Airbus Group, Company Annual Report 2016 (Airbus, 2017) http://company.airbus.com/investors/Annual-reports-and-registration-documents.html (last accessed 16 June 2017).
5. University of Cambridge Judge Business School, 'Company focus: what's it like working for Amazon?' (*News & Insights* Cambridge Judge Business School 27 April 2017) https://insight.jbs.cam.ac.uk/2017/company-focus-whats-it-like-working-for-amazon/ (last accessed 2 July 2017).
6. Caterpillar Inc, 'Powering the Future Sustainably' (Caterpillar Sustainability) http://www.caterpillar.com/nl/company/sustainability/innovation-technology.html (last accessed 2 July 2017).
7. Yury Boshyk, Business Driven Action Learning: Global Best Practices (Springer 2016) 97.
8. Rick Wartzman, 'Coke's leadership formula: Sending its rising star execs away for six weeks' (*Fortune* 14 May 2015) http://fortune.com/2015/05/14/coke-leadership-program/ (last accessed 3 July 2017).
9. Ethan Rouen, 'When leaders are scarce, employees look to peers' (*Fortune* 19 April 2012) http://fortune.com/2012/04/19/when-leaders-are-scarce-employees-look-to-peers/ (last accessed 20 February 2018).

10. David A. Clutterbuck, Frances K. Kochan, Laura Lunsford, Nora Dominguez and Julie Haddock-Millar, *The SAGE Handbook of Mentoring* (Sage 2017) 414.
11. Kevin Lusk, 'Thoughts for the C-Suite: why smart CEOs have a mentor' (*CME Manitoba* 5 May 2017) http://mb.cme-mec.ca/?action=show&lid=XE8MT-GCZX2-KAD9G&comaction=show&cid=V6EWB-XUK6T-QE6F4 (last accessed 21 March 2018).
12. Rob Leavitt, 'The Marketing Strategist: Cisco's Award-winning Thought Leadership: The Internet of Everything' (*ITSMA* 17 May 2016) https://www.itsma.com/cisco-award-winning-thought-leadership/ (last accessed 1 February 2018).
13. n2growth, 'Leadership matters: Interview with ex-Rio Tinto head Sam Walsh' (*Mining.com* 31 July 2016) www.mining.com/web/ex-rio-tinto-chief-on-why-mentors-are-vital/ (last accessed 30 November 2017).
14. D. L. Cooperrider and D. Whitney, 'Appreciative Inquiry: A positive revolution in change' in P. Holman and T. Devane (eds), *The Change Handbook* (Berrett-Koehler Publishers, Inc.) 245–63.
15. Ron Williams and Jon Spector, 'Here's how to develop millennials to become CEOs' (*World Economic Forum* 13 January 2017) https://www.weforum.org/agenda/2017/01/heres-how-to-develop-millennials-to-become-ceos (last accessed 30 November 2017).
16. BNY Mellon, 'Behind the Scenes with Darah Kirstein: Mentoring BNY Mellon's CEO' (BNY Mellon Behind the Scenes Series, 19 May 2016) https://www.bnymellon.com/us/en/newsroom/news/expert-voices/behind-the-scenes-with-darah-kirstein-mentoring-bny-mellons-ceo.jsp (last accessed 30 November 2017).
17. Microsoft Inc, 'Reverse mentoring: How millennials are becoming the new mentors' (Microsoft Central Europe, 2017) https://news.microsoft.com/europe/features/reverse-mentoring-how-millennials-are-becoming-the-new-mentors (last accessed 30 November 2017).
18. Ganesh Natarajan and Prameela Kalive, *From Start-Up to Global Success: The Zensar Story* (Sage 2016).
19. Derek du Preez, 'GE staying Current by becoming an 'as-a-service' business' (*Dogmatica* 17 June 2016) https://diginomica.com/2016/06/17/ge-staying-current-by-becoming-an-as-a-service-business/ (last accessed 30 November 2017).
20. Jill Dyche, 'The untold story: the power of corporate storytelling' (Financial Times Corporate Leaning Alliance 28 March 2017) http://www.ftiecla.com/2017/03/28/the-untold-story-the-power-of-corporate-storytelling/ (last accessed 30 November 2017).
21. Bill Goodwin, 'BP spends £2m developing apps to train business leaders' (*Computerweekly.com* 8 September 2014) <http://www.computerweekly.com/news/2240228335/BP-invests-2-million-in-apps-to-train-business-leaders (last accessed 30 November 2017).
22. Martin Reeves and Georg Wittenburg, 'Games can make you a better strategist' (*Harvard Business Review* 7 September 2015) https://hbr.org/2015/09/games-can-make-you-a-better-strategist (last accessed 10 January 2018).
23. Richard Feloni, 'Dropbox's CEO credits his success to a habit he's passed on to his executive team' (*Business Insider* 7 December 2017) http://www.businessinsider.de/why-dropboxs-leadership-team-reads-four-book-each-year-2017-12?r=UK&IR=T (last accessed 10 January 2018).

24. Microsoft Inc, 'Second version of HoloLens HPU will incorporate AI coprocessor for implementing DNNs, (*Microsoft Blog Graphics and Media* 23 July 2017) https://www.microsoft.com/en-us/research/blog/second-version-hololens-hpu-will-incorporate-ai-coprocessor-implementing-dnns/ (last accessed 10 January 2018).

25. Dean Takahashi, 'AdHawk's tiny sensors could enable much smaller VR headsets and AR glasses' (*Venture Beat* 19 October 2017) https://venturebeat.com/2017/10/19/adhawks-tiny-sensors-could-enable-much-smaller-vr-headsets-and-ar-glasses/amp/ (last accessed 10 January 2018).

26. Somo Global, 'Augmented reality product and multi-touch interactive table bring petro-technical training experiences to life' (Somo Global Press Release, 29 October 2014) https://blog.somoglobal.com/press-releases/somo-pioneers-immersive-interactive-learning-experience-for-bp (last accessed 1 January 2018).

Designing executive development to fit unique organisational needs

This chapter will address the importance of making executive development programmes work for organisations and avoiding the 'magic bullet' and 'one-size-fits-all' approaches which can be counterproductive and ineffective in driving the desired organisational impact and outcomes on business drivers. It will recap some of the content covered in previous chapters, but the focus will be reflective and address how executive development can be designed to align with the unique characteristics of the organisation, rather than offering a universal solution. Specific factors that will be addressed include organisational size considerations, learning needs assessment process for executives, how executive development can be tailored to address cultural climate challenges, sector dynamics and how appropriate digital technology and platforms can be effectively integrated into the learning architecture.

Size of organisation

The size of an organisation is a crucial factor in determining the scale and scope of the executive development interventions required to drive value and long-term growth. Some of the challenges that large organisations face including recommended modalities for addressing these challenges are outlined below:

- Slow responsiveness in changing the organisational value systems and structure in a timely manner to fend off disruptive businesses and innovators (*modalities:* mentoring/coaching from start-up entrepreneurs / disruptors from other sectors, seminars led by thought leaders on digital innovation and culture transformation related educational courses packed with compelling storytelling about how organisations have approached similar challenges to improve decision-making effectiveness).
- Presence of counterproductive sub-cultures hindering innovation and creativity which may be out of sync with the overarching organisational strategy (*modalities:* job rotation in high-performing areas of the business, site visits to exemplary divisions /locations (followed by action planning

and reflection), extensive executive coaching and mentoring led by senior leadership teams, exposure to peer networking to gain new insights and shadowing senior leadership teams to gain the gravitas/political capabilities to dismantle negative sub-cultures swiftly and build collation across key internal stakeholders to drive cultural transformation).

- Capital adequacy overconfidence, resulting in investment in non-value adding ventures (*modalities:* overconfidence bias training to ensure that investment decisions are thoroughly assessed and properly justified, interactive seminars by thought leaders/educational programmes/courses on portfolio analysis and financial economics focusing on cost/value sensitivity analysis, seminars led by venture capitalist and start-up entrepreneurs to imbibe mindset/discipline of delivering innovative solutions with limited resources and competitor analysis for comparable insight).

- Differential performance across divisions, geographic location and business units (modalities: job rotation/shadowing peers in high-performing divisions/units, coaching and mentoring delivered by senior leaders, focusing on building capacity in troubleshooting and productivity improvement, learning through community of practice and knowledge share, delivered via technology for convenience, and speed dating events/regular internal networking events to validate and test assumptions with peers).

- Over-reliance of debt financing and mergers to rapidly expand business with limited value creation (*modalities:* thought leaders/experts seminars/talks/educational programmes on financial economics to improve merger and acquisition expertise, merger and acquisition simulations focusing on trade-off analysis to improve decision-making effectiveness, coaching/training programmes on effective decision-making to address groupthink/herding behaviours within the executive cohort, developing capabilities on merger and acquisition through less risky/smaller deals before moving into more complex ones and enhancing innovation and business growth mindset through interactions with venture capitalist and start-up entrepreneurs to optimise organic growth opportunities, and provision of coaching and mentoring of the executive team by seasoned/retired CEOs with solid mergers and acquisitions experience).

- Decline in risk appetite, experimentation and risk-taking behaviour to drive the innovation and creativity across all divisions, departments and geographical regions (*modalities:* seminars/presentations led by disruptive innovators and entrepreneurs to stimulate start-up mentality and growth mindset, high-performance coaching to drive goal-orientation, reverse mentoring to stimulate effective ideation from the younger generation population of the workforce, involving executives in 'internal' hackathon to building decision-making speed and experimentation capabilities, cross-functional/cross-geographic projects specifically aimed at developing disruptive solutions and business models to move executives outside their comfort zones delivered within compressed timescales to stimulate risk-taking behaviours).

- Limited interdepartmental cooperation and silo mentality hindering innovation, creativity and development of products and services to enhance customer experience (*modalities*: cross departmental hackathons to build internal collations and collaborative mindset, engaging in projects/ assignments that involves working with ecosystem partners to break silo mentality and then transferring this internally to foster collaborative working with peers, speed dating/showcase events to gain insight into complexities/interconnectivity/pain-points of other functions and internal networking events to build collations across departments and joint interactions with customers to gain collective insight on developing unique solutions to enhance customer experience).
- Decision ineffectiveness and delays in strategy implementation owing to incongruent organisational structures and systems (*modalities*: coaching and mentoring programmes to enable the swift spotting and dismantling of political blockers, emotional intelligence training to deal with difficult employees, employee engagement training to enhance the level of staff motivation across departments, inclusivity and unconsciousness bias training to broaden the contributions from marginalised sections of the workforce, communication training supported by group coaching sessions to ensure that messages and behaviours exhibited by the executive cohort is clear, consistent and congruent with organisational strategy.

Small and medium-sized firms will be less prone to some of the structural drag which stifles creativity and innovation in larger organisations but face other unique challenges, which will feed into the design of executive development programmes such as:

- Limited funds and resource constraints resulting in delayed product launch (*modalities*: participating in ecosystems with larger organisations to build capabilities to launch partnerships, reading books/blogs/attending seminars about building investor/business angel relationships, reading books/listening to podcasts on building communication/negotiations skills to secure funding from business angels, venture capitalist and larger organisation, and developing networking capabilities to tap into innovative funding sources to grow business).
- Growth challenges – too fast into self-destruction mode (i.e. too fast and therefore not sustainable) or too slow to cause organisational decline (*modalities*: simulations to test assumptions/trade-offs and implications, visits to successful organisations in different sectors to understand obstacles/ traps to growth, coaching and mentoring from executives in larger organisations, podcast/seminars/short courses on financial analysis/analytics to prepare for sustainable growth, courses and training/seminars on

investment options including mergers, acquisitions including other forms of partnership to determine best pathways for growth).

- Developing the company culture during expansion into other markets (*modalities*: simulations to assess the implications of countercultural tendencies on organisational outcomes, competitors analysis to learn from others who have been successful in this area, training/podcasts/ books on diversity management and cultural integrations, learning through network/contacts situated in prospective markets, visits to non-competitors in the prospective markets, and unconsciousness bias training to avoid cultural clashes in target markets).
- Groupthink owing to relatively small executive cohort, which can result in ineffective decision-making (*modalities*: unconsciousness bias training, coaching and mentoring from executives in larger organisations, reverse mentoring with executives in larger organisations, team reflection sessions facilitated by external parties, and training/ podcast/ blogs on decision-making effectiveness).
- Organisational design during expansion and to maximise disruption (*modalities:* coaching from executives in larger organisations, books/ courses on/podcasts on effective organisational design, learning, reverse mentoring from senior executives in larger organisations, and learning from peers in network).
- Market selection, speed of penetration and optimising the impact of these events on financial position (*modalities:* simulations to confirm/disconfirm assumptions, coaching from executives in larger organisations, courses, training/podcasts on marketing, and competitor analysis and intelligence).

Sector-specific dynamics and challenges

The design of executive development programmes needs to take into account specific sector dynamics and challenges as there are always some unique factors which drive the business models, profit margins, and value drivers. Even the impact of megatrends such as automation and machine learning is likely to disrupt certain industries and sectors much faster than others so the speed of learning and repositioning of business models will need to be accelerated to match.

Another crucial reason why sector dynamics needs to be integrated into the executive development design process is that there is variability in the maturity levels of executive development across sectors, which has implications on executive development in terms of the design and implementation processes. According to a Harvard Business research, the most matured 7 per cent executive development programmes are delivered by large publicly listed companies in the aerospace, consumer goods, financial services and pharmaceuticals industries with over 10,000 employees, whilst the underperforming

13 per cent are located within the construction, professional services and retail industries and tend to be privately held companies with fewer than 5,000 employees.[1] This implies that executive development in the underperforming sectors should take a more nurturing approach as discussed in Chapter 3 for less matured organisations.

Some of the industry-specific challenges that may need to be addressed through executive development – including possible solutions – are discussed in the following section.

Pharmaceutical: Within this sector, challenges include the prolonged drug development process and huge R&D expenditure,[2] intellectual property challenges stemming from cloning of products by Third World drug producers, and failed strategies in extending existing models into non-traditional pharma markets – all of which put pressure on the capacity to generate value and long-term growth.[3] Solutions include developing collaborative capabilities to engage with start-up AI firms to explore means of accelerating production processes; engaging in curated learning and experiential learning to develop understanding of local cultural drivers to set sustainable pricing strategies; and gaining understanding of legal processes through immersive interactions with politicians via pro bono assignments.

Bringing a new pharmaceutical drug to market takes several years and can reach into the billions in R&D expenditures, and so industry leaders are now seeking more efficient methods of approaching this process and machine learning is emerging as a potential solution. This will require executives to grasp the principles of AI, Deep Learning and Machine Learning and the implication on R&D process and other areas of the business. Executives can also learn by conducting industry level trends analysis and by comparing and contrasting direct and indirect competitor best practices in the area of machine learning applications to benefit from this technology. Another suitable approach is for executives in this sector to engage coaches with machine learning background to help them develop insight and guide them through the possible frontiers, limitations and challenges associated with implementing this technology in this sector.

Executives will also need to develop capabilities that will enable them to synthesis the contributions of ecosystem partners, and AI experts, to align with corporate strategy and to drive effective cross-functional, collaboration across leadership levels to successfully design and deliver projects to improve the drug development processes.

Mining: Mining companies are facing the challenge of driving innovation and disruption in order to drive down debt levels, whilst maintaining environmental and safety standards in a sector that has – until recently – not been associated with innovation. The rapid introduction of technology such as autonomous trains, trucks, drilling and mining equipment – driven by AI, robotics and emerging technologies – means that future mining executives will need to develop stronger collaborative working capabilities to work with their industry partners and suppliers, and build wider ecosystem partnerships to introduce ground-breaking innovation to address productivity challenges.

Executives in the mining sector need to become more adept at allocating capital, delivery of capital projects, dealing with geopolitical issues (including hostile government relations and local demands) and addressing talent gaps in the executive suite and below.[4]

Relations with governments across the world are becoming more hostile as they aggressively continue to increase their ownership of mine revenue with countries such as DRC, Tanzania South Africa, the Philippines, and Brazil all vying for an increasing share of the revenues generated from mineral resources.

For example, in Tanzania mining companies such as Acacia Mining, Petra Diamonds and Kibo Mining face increasing challenges following the introduction of new laws that allow the government to renegotiate or revoke existing contracts aimed at increasing the share of revenue generated from the country's natural resources.[5]

Development interventions to address innovation and collaboration gaps include training and experiential activities to embed start-up mentality, extensive tours/learning exchange with technology companies, vertical and horizontal job rotation across departments to build collaborative working capabilities and learn from ecosystem partners outside the industry to inject creative ideas necessary for expanding innovation capabilities.

Rio Tinto's foray into autonomous freight trains, trucking, drilling technologies and other innovative initiatives driven by the 'mine of the future' concept has been successfully delivered by the executives and other organisational leaders working with broader range ecosystem systems partners. For instance, the successful implementation of the autonomous train technology was developed and implemented in partnership with a number of organisations including Hitachi and Ansaldo STS Technology.[6] This underpins the importance of mining executives building the capability of working in a broader ecosystem to develop innovation successfully in both the technological front and in addressing safety challenges in this sector.

Barrick Mining is another company driving innovations with input from outside the mining sector through ecosystem partnerships to address business challenges and through a series of hackathons, organised across a number of countries such as the US, UK, Australia and China, which serves as a development activity for executives to gain capabilities to drive innovation across the organisation.[7]

Senior leaders from Caterpillar Inc., BHP and Gekko organise regular visits to Silicon Valley in San Francisco, where they interact with corporate venture capitalist, accelerators and start-ups in other sectors to learn how to adapt the ecosystem model to launch innovative technology in the mining industry.[8] A similar approach can be taken by other mining executives with existing/new partners to develop innovation hubs with start-ups where executives can develop the capacity to launch and nurture innovative solutions to some of the challenges confronting the mining sector.

To address the challenge of dealing with government and demands from local stakeholders, mining executives' development programmes need to build their negotiating ability, cultural sensitivity and influencing skills. Executive coaching targeted at personal adaptability will be particularly useful in helping executives to better sense and adjust to changes, and to engage, manage and deal with politicians and local groups. To address the talent gap, the executive development provision should be widened to include lower level managers, and coaching programmes should be developed so that senior executives can provide coaching to lower level managers. Finally, educational programmes on efficient capital allocation; simulations and immersive learning programmes on capital project delivery; and learning exchange programmes with industries that are more efficient at delivery of capital programmes, will be useful considerations in the design of executive development in the mining sector.

Oil and gas sectors: Some of the challenges in this sector include intensifying competition from non-fossil sources such as wind, solar and other renewable source, increased competition within the sector driven owing to the desire to optimise extraction of deposits at a lower cost by developing solutions through artificial intelligence and robotics; shrinking global geoscience and engineering talent pools; increasing societal awareness of environmental risks; complexities in managing the upstream business ecosystem; and managing health, safety, security and environmental (HSSE) considerations in the multinational corporation and throughout the business environment.[9]

Executives in this sector need to develop the capacity to drive innovation in today's low-price market to survive and disrupt through automation, robotics and artificial intelligence.[10] The decline in the reliance on fossil fuels with the emergence of battery-propelled vehicles and alternative energy suppliers such as solar, wind, geothermal, biomass, tidal, and wave energy is driving cost pressures in this sector.

Development interventions that will be relevant to executives in this sector include engaging and dealing with difficult stakeholders outside the normal remit to prepare them for future challenges, networking and collaborative interventions to work in a broader ecosystem, diversity management, employee engagement and unconscious bias training to manage multicultural talent base. Development interventions involving working with start-ups and developing start-up mind-set, educational programmes on strategies for dealing with disruptive start-ups, experiential learning to strengthen the capacity of executives to work with partners outside the core industry to launch innovative technology and new business models to counteract the declining revenues posed by alternative energy suppliers will also be beneficial to executives in this sector.

Equinor (formerly known as Statoil) created a model for executive development suitable for mid-level executives to build their capability in managing mega opportunities, which can be replicated by other players in the sector. The structure of the development programme, which was aimed at expanding participants capability in handling challenging stakeholders, complexity and decision effectiveness was designed as an immersive and challenging learning experience requiring participants to create a journal of their experiences to evoke a reflective practice, culminating in a debriefing session to senior executives. The programme also involved working in a different industrial setting and interacting with politicians, local businesses, community leaders and a wider scope of stakeholders to broaden the exposure of participants to encompass how to anticipate and integrate the concerns and needs of wider stakeholders in analysing mega projects.[11]

If designed effectively, the above development approach can assist executives to develop multiple capabilities concurrently including, the capacity to handle difficult stakeholders outside the normal remit; improved networking and collaborative capacity by working in a much wider ecosystem; becoming more self-aware and thereby minimise unconscious bias through reflective practice and interacting with local communities; and enhancing decision effectiveness through consensus building and consideration of wider factors, including geopolitical issues, which can impact on value creation.

Utilities: Traditional utility sector firms face a number of challenges including the growth in market share of renewable energy, challenging economics of traditional power generation plants (high cost of ageing assets), decline in demand owing to the introduction of energy efficient appliances, changing customer experience and preferences (switching to greener and cheaper alternatives), pressure of regulatory bodies resulting in downwards adjustment in prices.[12]

Some of the possible solutions to the challenges faced by traditional utilities includes expanding into service provision and co-creation of digital devices and with ecosystem partners. Some of the digital devices which can be explored through partnership arrangements include smart devices (for domestic – lights, thermostats etc and industrial customers – automation, sensors, and intelligent energy grid systems) and energy efficient appliances and installation of electric charging networks for electric vehicles.

In terms of service provision, utility firms can expand their business models to include energy efficiency consulting to manufacturing and industries with high consumption, energy measurement and audit, bill management systems for small renewables generators, energy exchange with renewables suppliers, management of maintenance of electric charging stations and financing of start-ups in the renewable sector. Expansion of the business models will require executives to develop new capabilities to minimise potential failures as they move into unchartered territories.

EnBW, a German-based utility company, has been expanding its business model from the traditional generation base to encompass both service provision and digital devices. The expansion into service delivery is achieved by offering improvement in service quality and financial management to existing and other energy companies and municipalities as well as working on a range of digital products based on a smart city concept developed with ecosystem partners.[13] All of these initiatives are bolstered by an innovation campus established to foster the development of new technological offerings by providing key employees within all departments, including executives with the right capabilities to accelerate the benefit realisation process, including the launching of internal start-ups and working more effectively with creative ecosystems partners.

Another example of a utility company expanding its business model away from the traditional business model is the US-based Exelon, which has established a dedicated venturing division to invest in innovative energy technologies such as Aquion Energy (a sustainable saltwater battery solution), and Proterra (developing the technology for a zero-emission electric city bus) and helping these portfolio companies grow by providing them capital and management expertise to overcome some of the marketing and expansion-related challenges faced by smaller organisations.[14]

In addition, Exelon has launched a programme dubbed 'Dancing with the Startups', which provides a platform for the organisation to foster relationships with startups, venture capitalists and the academic community to validate new business models, test new technologies and to embed an innovative mindset within its organisation structure.[15]

This offers executives the capability to develop a start-up mind-set as they work, grow and integrate these new ventures into the main business portfolio, expanding the revenue model as well as providing development opportunities for emerging talent to broaden their experience by working outside the core power generation sector.

US-based utility provider NRG is also evolving its business model to a more robust and future-proof one by gradually augmenting the traditional generation assets with renewable energy, development of electric vehicles and micro grids (solar, wind and battery powered) with ecosystem partners.[16]

Other modalities to be included in the design of executive development to address some of the challenges faced by utility sector executives include educational programmes on strategic cost reduction, learning through simulations to enhance the ability to better evaluate various business models to counteract the increasing interventions from regulatory bodies, networking and collaborative learning modalities to enable executives to initiate the co-creation of complimentary products and services with partners outside the utilities sector, and interventions which can engender a start-up mentality for creating disruptive products.

Retail sector: The retail sector faces a number of challenges, which include ever-changing customer experience and greater need for customisation (including the shift towards digital platforms), significantly lower staff engagement and retention levels compared to other sectors, and the threat posed by the emergence of low cost disruptors.

Development interventions should target how to address the challenges of an ever-changing customer experience and may include a blended learning approach (educational, experiential and networking, which was discussed into detail in the previous chapter) to creating compelling omni-channel value models – including interactive seminars led by thought leaders/leading academic to enable executives to master the development of effective KPIs for tracking and improving customer experience (such as expediting issue resolution, reducing average handle time, increasing first-time-resolution of customer issues), improving in-store conversion rates and cross-sell/upsell opportunities.[17]

However, executives in this sector tend to focus more attention on developing capabilities through traditional learning modules, often at the expense of other learning approaches. It has been observed that retailers have not yet explored a broader mix of technology-driven learning techniques with fewer retailers investing in blended learning (which is far below the average investment across all other sectors).[18]

A focus on coaching, unconscious bias training, and emotional intelligence training will also be beneficial in addressing some of the retention and engagement challenges prevalent in the retail sector These modalities can potentially highlight the behaviour patterns driving the disengagement levels and provide possible solutions for creating and maintaining higher levels of employee engagement. Unconsciousness bias can unearth patterns of behaviours that impact on engagement levels and how these can be addressed. Emotional Intelligence training for example can increase executive self and social awareness of their emotional responses in different situations and scenarios and they can improve the interactions with peers and employees by considering the possible implications of their actions and inactions.[19] Coaching can provide executives with the necessary stretch goals, value systems and behaviour adjustments and reflection required to move to a highly engaged level.

IBM, for example, has made emotional intelligence assessment as an integral component of its coaching and mentoring development interventions delivered to their executive and management cohorts and the correlation between the emotional intelligence of participants and observed improvement in employee engagement and performance levels have been positive.[20]

Another avenue for developing the capabilities of executives in the retail sector is to engage in site visits (with follow-up coaching/mentoring sessions from peer executives) to other industries such as manufacturing, aviation and automobile sectors as a means of developing insights into the successful implementation of agile logistics operations to drive down operational costs.

Construction: The construction sector has been subject to poor productivity and thin profit margins, project performance issues, skills shortages and potential digital disrupters through the introduction of more efficient working practices supported by automation, robotics, AI and machine learning, thereby lowering the barriers of entry in this market such as has occurred in the auto industry by Tesla. In addition, it has been reported that executives and managers in the construction sector have limited people skills, which are required to drive employee engagement, talent management and innovation – but investment in development in this sector tends to focus on health and safety and organisational processes and procedures.[21]

Start-ups technology companies like Australian-based Fastbrick Robotics and US-originated ICON are blazing the trail in combining 3D technology and robotics to disrupt the building industry. Fastbrick Robotics has already secured investment from Caterpillar Inc. and has developed a 3D robotic bricklaying system, called the Hadrian X, to construct houses by applying laser guided technology to lay bricks accurately at an equivalent of 1,000 bricks per hour.[22] ICON is also employing advanced robotics and cutting-edge materials to provide sustainable and affordable housing solutions across the globe.[23]

The emergence of these two companies epitomises the level of disruption that will continue to challenge the norms and business models which will require construction executives to develop their capabilities by building innovation capabilities internally or forge relationships with a wider ecosystem in order to engineer disruptive technologies and solutions congruent with the emerging digital revolution.

Owing to cost pressures in this sector, low-cost executive development modalities can be used – including building innovation capabilities and decision-making capabilities through ecosystem partnerships, learning from peers (cross-sector) via networking interventions and events, curated eLearning content focused on broadening relational and social skills, rotational assignments (managed effectively not to impact on project delivery), internal coaching /mentoring from executives outside the industry to inject fresh perspectives and to challenge groupthink and silo mentality, and pro bono assignments with charitable organisations and reverse coaching (similar to reverse mentoring where executives at different levels exchange ideas/ experiences for mutual benefit) with start-up executives in other sectors (such as within the AI and related technology sector) to develop start-up mentality to drive innovation. All of these avenues can help executives in the construction sector to build people-centred capabilities required to enhance productivity and engagement levels and to also drive innovation through drive cross-departmental initiates and with ecosystem partnerships forged outside the construction industry.

Executive development in the construction sector should also focus on how to foster swift innovation across all levels of the organisation to develop technology and best practices, which will improve margins by increasing productivity levels, eliminating waste and addressing sustainability concerns.

In sum, there are unique sector/industry characteristics which determine/ influence the range of challenges that need to be addressed through executive development programmes. This also impacts on the level of additional budget required for development interventions and consideration of how rapidly the capability gaps and required changes can be implemented to keep up with changes in the wider sector and to fend off the competition posed by disruptive innovators.

Organisational culture maturity

Organisational culture encompasses the totality of shared value systems, accepted norms and prevailing behaviours which evolve over time through interaction with complex macro and micro sub-systems. Culture can be formed over time by the interaction of groups and individuals influenced by a complex web of unique macro factors at the national, regional, social, technological, economic, educational, industry, and knowledge levels. Micro factors such as geographic separation, professions and communities of practices, management styles, and departmental structures have an equally important effect on organisational culture. Executives can influence the prevailing culture by setting the values and behavioural models which can be reinforced through acceptance and replication by other leaders and then eventually become embedded across the organisation. The prevailing and evolving organisational culture can present a number of challenges, which need to be addressed through effective executive development design as detailed below.

Culture lagging with customer experience: As organisational culture evolves, it can either enable better adaptation to emerging challenges or lead to decline in performance owing to lack of synchronicity between organisational culture and customer expectations. Customer experience/expectations maturity levels can be assessed by considering some leading indicators such as; the awareness of employees about the top-five customer issues and channels for contributing possible solutions, levels of resources commitment to investigating and resolving the root causes of critical customer pain points, number of successful cross-functional initiatives created to pre-empt customer challenges, number of successful initiatives deployed to enhance deeper personalisation and customer experience. The assessment will determine the customer experience related modalities executives need to address any gaps.

Incongruence of sub-cultures: Since different functions of an organisation interact with different stakeholders/environments, there is a tendency for sub-cultures to emerge which may be counterproductive to the prevailing state required to drive value and growth. Sometimes these sub-cultures can co-exist within the wider organisational culture but, in some instances, these can stifle collaboration and cross-fertilisation of ideas across the organisation. This issue can be addressed by ensuring that executive development design provide executives with the diagnostic tools to identify these counter-productive sub-cultures, as well as the means to dismantle them without causing upheavals in the organisational settings in which such cultures are identified. Interventions such as team coaching/mentoring by external peer executives/retired executives and presentations from thought leaders/leading experts will be useful to address this challenge.

Cross-cultural and diversity misalignment: As the pace of business environmental change intensifies, the need to embrace diversity, experimentation and a multicultural employee base is crucial for adapting the organisational structure to enable the creation of products and services that deepen customer experience. But this quest for diversity can increase internal tensions and cultural clashes and hinder wider integration of accepted organisational culture and values. Design of executive development programmes must focus here on managing across cultures and building collaboration and consensus in competing cultural environments. In essence, executive development design must take into account how executives can become adept at articulating and reinforcing any new common adaptive values whilst managing the increasing diversity across the organisation.

Breaking hierarchical cultures: Breaking hierarchical mindsets and cultures is a very challenging endeavour which requires executives to reflect on their own approach as well as other leaders', within their immediate span of control. Engaging in interventions such as executive coaching /mentoring (for building the gravitas and diplomacy to diffuse tensions which may arise in the course of dismantling hierarchical mindsets), unconsciousness bias/diversity and inclusion training (to encourage leaders to expand the decision-making envelope beyond a 'selected few' executives) and collective team reflective practice (to consolidate/embed new inclusive behaviours), executives can break hierarchical barriers and allow employees at all levels to challenge enthroned positions, creating the positive collisions necessary for shifting the culture towards a more inclusive state.[24] The aim is to shift the hierarchical culture to an interdependent leadership culture where leadership is considered to be a collective activity that stimulates mutual inquiry, critical thinking, double loop learning (adjustment of mind-sets, behaviours, goals and decision-making patterns based on new experience and observations), and readies the organisation for addressing complex challenges.[25] Organisations must recognise that there is no permanent state of collaboration owing to attrition and other dynamic effects which impinge on organisational life. Hence, executives must develop the diagnostic capabilities or identifying the early warning signs of cultural decline as well as the political gravitas/diplomacy necessary for adapting and evolving the organisational culture to align with changing external business challenges and opportunities.

Executive development needs analysis

Taking time to unearth the drivers and motivations for engaging in development interventions – as well as the gaps in the current capabilities – may not be popular with executive cohorts, but this is an important exercise which – if carried out effectively – can feed into the business case for the executive development programmes, and help determine the best modalities or intervention to adopt for both individual and team executives, including aggregation of delivery modalities to achieve economies of scale, depending on organisational size. For example, if the need for a common coaching intervention is identified through HR data analytics, the delivery can be contracted out to a single consulting firm to generate efficiencies, instead of using different entities which can be more expensive and complex to manage. The development needs analysis process can also serve as the cornerstone for planning/assessing the data requirements for the post-implementation return on investment evaluation stage.

Executive development needs analysis can be carried out using the steps shown in figure 4.1 below, starting from the identification and mapping of value drivers, capability gap analysis, establishment of delivery mechanisms and finally, selection of impact assessment and concluding with the consideration of return of investment indicators.

Mapping of value drivers and challenges: This process should encompass identification of the current and future value drivers required to generate sustainable value and growth, as well as any broad industry level challenges and any gap between the organisation and competitors along the value chain. Consideration should also be given to mapping of any threat posed by emerging disruptors and innovators across the value chain, including any emerging megatrends, customer trends, internal operational deficiencies, and regulatory changes that will impact on the ability of the organisation to achieve its sustainable growth targets.

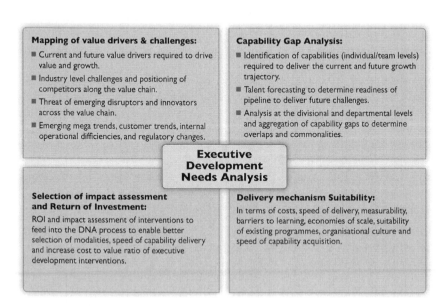

Figure 4.1 Executive Development Needs Analysis.

Capability gap analysis: This step will involve the identification of capabilities (individual/team levels) required to deliver the current and future growth trajectory, and this process is likely to be most effective where individual executives/teams demonstrate greater degrees of openness, honesty, self-awareness, and willingness to accept change, all of which are driven by the prevailing organisational culture. Talent forecasting must also be undertaken at this stage to determine the readiness of the pipeline to deliver future challenges at the divisional and departmental levels, including aggregation of capability gaps to determine overlaps and commonalities.

Once the capability gap analysis process is completed, it is beneficial for the learning and development department to map out, in consultation with executives, the possible interventions that can be employed to close identified gaps, as well as consideration of the range of intangible and tangible measures which will be used to determine the return on investment assessment computations. At this stage, only a high-level consideration of these factors will suffice to ensure early buy-in from executives regarding suitability of measures, frequency and ease of data collection, level of support required from other departments/divisions and any existing/new technological platforms which can be employed to store and analyse the information.

In order to manage the expectations of executives during the gap analysis stage, it is important to position this process as part of a development journey which can be illustrated via the 5-As development model depicted in figure 4.2.

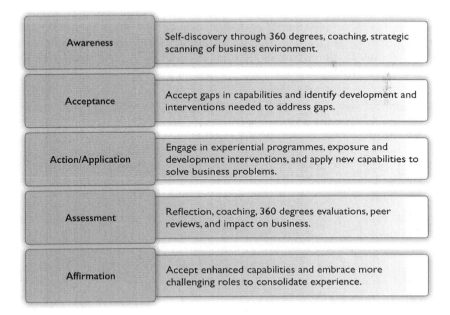

Figure 4.2 The 5-As Individual Executive development model.

The initial step of the 5A model involves the individual executive gaining awareness of any gaps in their current capabilities by engaging in 360-degree evaluations, coaching, strategic scanning of the business environment, and identifying trends and new business models in other sectors. This will then lead to openness and recognition of the gaps and limitations in capabilities so that an adequate level of development intervention can be selected to close this gap. The individual executive must then assume accountability for the actions required to close the capability gap, including deepening their experiences by engaging in suitable development interventions, and looking for opportunities to apply the new capabilities to solve business problems. It is important to note the connection between the identification of individual capabilities and that of the team to reiterate the previously highlighted point that a culture of openness creates a conducive environment for individuals to feel more comfortable about discussing their own development needs. The effectiveness of the development interventions need to be assessed by suitable lagging and leading indicators and corrective measures must be implemented until desired outcomes are achieved. To consolidate and embed the new capabilities gained through the development processes, executives need to accept this new level of performance/capability and seek more challenging roles to exert their full potential to drive organisational value. Whilst this model is focused on the individual level, it can also be applied at the executive team level, in team coaching scenarios, as it offers a simplistic and structured approach to developing and embedding learning in an organisational setting.

Delivery mechanism suitability: This involves the consideration of interrelated factors to assess the suitability of learning mechanism such as direct and indirect costs, economies of scale opportunities, speed of delivery, measurability of outcomes, barriers to learning transfer /application, suitability of existing programmes, organisational culture readiness and speed of capability acquisition. Larger organisations are more likely to derive more benefit from consolidating development interventions to gain economies of scale compared to smaller counterparts, by leveraging higher participants numbers to negotiate lower rates with training providers and educational institutions. The speed of delivery needs to be aligned with existing commitments of participants including milestones/timeline for which the desired capability is expected to be embedded and deployed to drive value creation. Assessment of the measurability of the interventions is equally important in determining the suitability of the delivery mechanism as it assists in early planning and monitoring of data collection required for the return of investment (ROI) analysis stage. Identification of the possible barriers to learning, transfer and application needs to be considered at both the individual and team levels and possible solutions should be developed to address these challenges. Some possible barriers which need to be considered, include busy lifestyle of participants and the likely impact on absorption/retention capacity, lack of learning application/transfer opportunities, and incongruent internal organisational

cultures that can stifle the speed of learning transfer. A review of the suitability of existing programmes against possible changes in the demographic
composition, educational levels, and professional backgrounds of the executive cohorts is likely to impact on the preference for certain modalities (e.g.
younger generation may prefer more technology-based delivery compared to
older counterparts who may opt for more interactive approaches). Speed of
capability acquisition must take into account the individual's unique learning
preferences, workload, and other behavioural characteristics to ensure that
adequate support such as mentoring and coaching can be offered to embed
any newly acquired capabilities. Relatedly, the DNA process also needs to
evaluate the 'engagement quotient' attached to the selected modality. i.e. the
degree to which learners are likely to be connected to the selected modality, as people respond to learning interventions differently. If this issue is
not sufficiently addressed, there is a tendency for participants to be disen-
gaged, thereby reduce the viability for transferability and application to drive
changes in organisational processes which will negate the purpose for investments in the development interventions.

According to Kolb's Learning Style Inventory adult learners can be categorised into four dominant sets: Accommodator (inclined to learn by feeling
and doing – activist); Assimilator (has the proclivity to learn by thinking
and watching – theorist); Diverger (has the tendency to learn by feeling and
watching – reflector); and Converger (has the propensity to engage in thinking and doing while learning -pragmatist), all of which needs to be taken into
account in designing and personalising and increasing the range and variety
of experiences which can be offered through different executive development
interventions to maximise return on investments.[26]

Development interventions that may be more suitable for each dominant
learning style applicable to the executive cohort are outlined as follows.
Accommodators, owing to their inclination to learn by feeling and doing
(activist), will have the preference for action-learning, risk taking, experimentation, special projects, creative ventures, working with start-ups and
therefore have less inclination towards instructed-led training. On the other
hand, assimilators, who have the proclivity to learn by thinking and watching (theorist), can learn better from expert opinions, thought-leaders, and
logical reasoning and are therefore likely to prefer modalities such as learning
through networking with peers, communities of practices, expert opinions,
attending conference and other forms of modalities with a high degree of interaction but may have lower preference for practically inclined development
interventions. Divergers have the tendency to learn by feeling and watching
(reflector) and hence will feel more comfortable in engaging in reflective
activities, working with others and then having time to ponder over events
and will therefore have more preference for development intervention such
as simulations, listening to podcast, reading books, reflective thinking and
coaching. Finally, convergers have the tendency to engage in thinking and

doing while learning (pragmatist), therefore these individuals may have the propensity to combine both practical experience, interactions and validation of ideas and hence development interventions that combine networking and experiential development interventions, such as job rotations, field trips, and learning in an ecosystem setting will be most suitable for this cohort of learners.

For example, a study which examined the influence of learning styles on the learners' intentions to use technology-based learning content such as MOOCs revealed that learners with a high-reflective learning style (or convergers) have a lesser preference and therefore limited engagement with this approach of learning compared to others, especially where there is limited practical connection and lack of opportunity to validate concepts and ideas whilst engaging in this type of development intervention.[27]

This limitation can be addressed by ensuring that executive participants with the converger learning style are made aware of this tendency and the connection with business values should be made much clearer to this cohort to minimise the levels of disengagement.

Impact and return on investment assessment: The last step in the executive development needs analysis process involves conducting a high-level ROI and impact assessment of the selected interventions to enable selection of the most effective modalities and to priorities/accelerate the speed of delivery of interventions by ranking them according to the highest cost-to-value ratio. Some leading indicators can be identified (see Chapter 7 for examples of leading indicators) at this stage for each modality to determine the ease of measurement and to determine how data will be collected to measure the impact of executive development interventions on organisational outcomes, which is detailed in Chapter 7.

Use of digital technology/platforms

Owing to the nature and pace of executive work, there is a huge benefit in employing digital platforms to provide synchronous and asynchronous, just-in-time and micro learning to address capability gaps as these digital learning platforms fit around the work pattern of executives and are accessible over multiple devices. Some of the potential gaps that executives can close through this approach include insights on AI, deep learning, machine learning, virtual reality, and other emerging areas of digital technology.

Digital learning platforms can enable executives to gain access to insightful webinars, listen to podcasts on various business topics, join peers in virtual classrooms, gain access to the knowledge and expertise of leading professionals, and collaborate with peers in delivering challenging role-based and work-based projects with minimal interruption to their work.[28]

The learning, application and reflection dairies can also be recorded and tracked, enabling a large population of leaders across the organisation to access a shared learning repository, which will also be helpful for determining the best modalities and content for improving the capabilities of emerging leaders.[29] Analysis of the cumulated data will also flag ineffective content, approaches and modalities, and will help to map out any potential preferences – at the individual, geographic and cultural levels – in engaging with different learning methods.

However, the emphasis of employing technological platforms should be on enhancing transfer and application of learning and, ultimately, the strategic alignment of learning to business needs instead of innovation in delivery or providing sheer volumes of curated content to learners. The degree to which organisations can integrate digital technology and platforms (including curated learning content) into their executive development design process depends on a number of factors such as executive team's cultural maturity in terms of embracing digital technology, scalability of the development modality across a number of executive cohorts, level of personalisation required by participants and the breadth of complementary development offerings accessible within the organisation.

Digital culture maturity levels: Investing in digital technologies and platforms will yield limited results if the executive cohort have limited digital skills or do not perceive this to be a preferred modality for acquiring the targeted capability. To combat this challenge, reverse mentoring (which was discussed in Chapter 3) can be utilised to prepare executives to embrace digital technology ahead of implementation of such technologies. In addition to this, the design should incorporate more bite-sized delivery with regular pauses to allow for reflection, recap and application to specific business challenges to increase the levels of retention and application. Also, the level of digital culture maturity (assessed by the degree to which a digital mind-set is embraced and integrated into organisational vision values, and structure to drive effective ecosystem business models to generate enhanced customer experience) of executive cohorts can determine if the design of learning programmes should contain non-personalised curated (sporadically collection of digital learning resources), personalised curated (targeted collection of digital resources) or full-blown digital solution (content and delivery delivered mainly via digital technology platforms).

For example, Accenture, in collaboration with MIT, has designed a Technology Executive Development Programme, which is interactive and delivered entirely on a virtual platform (spanning multiple time zones) to meet the needs of high-potential technology managers. It offers participants a unique opportunity to interact with Accenture technology leaders, Accenture Global Delivery Network MIT Sloan faculty and other participants located across a wide geographic region.[30]

The platform has interactive features such as breakout rooms where participants can engage in small-group discussion, verbal reporting (similar to classroom environments), and employs virtual whiteboards for recording findings and comments, which are visible to all group members. These features are also augmented by a chat box functionality, which allows for a consistent flow of comments that faculty or other participants can quickly react to, and instant polling functionality helps to gauge participants' grasp of specific topics.[31] It should be noted that this approach is a high-cost solution which may not be suitable for all organisations and therefore a cost-benefit analysis needs to be undertaken as part of the development needs analysis process to determine the suitability of this approach to address gaps in executive development.

Scalability of the development modality: The economies of scale and impact that can be gained from curated digital content from online learning programmes offered by providers including Coursera, Degreed, Declara, Cross-Knowledge Harvard Online, Lynda.com, Virtual Ashridge and Udemy, can generate limited value if they stand to benefit only a small number of executives (economies of scale was previously discussed in this chapter but here the concept is contextualised within the space of curated digital content). An effective needs analysis process – including the consolidation of gaps across the organisation – is crucial in determining the value of selecting specific curated content and ensuring alignment of this content with the capabilities the organisation wants executives to develop.

Level of personalisation required by participants:

Although curated content can be developed from different types of applications and platforms such as videos, podcasts and presentations, allowing for a personalised learning experience is key in extracting the maximum benefit from investing in digital learning platforms. Personalisation of the content is motivational in terms of meeting people's specific learning preferences and therefore potentially increases knowledge retention and applicability.

Some curated content may not meet the unique needs of executives and may be generic as the instructors cannot pre-empt the background of the business to provide relevant solutions – which therefore limits the level of transferability. To address some of these limitations, organisations can work with vendors to customise the content of digital learning platforms to align with their internal processes and specific organisational needs. This approach is much more expensive (and therefore must be subject to a cost benefit analysis to justify the investment) as it requires establishing intellectual property agreements with vendors, but has the benefit of providing development and learning solutions that are relevant to learners' needs as it allows the infusion of company-specific terminologies, industry specific examples, and compelling story-telling scenarios relevant to various levels of the executive cohorts, all of which can be tied up with the specific value drivers that the organisation wants to enhance to support the accelerated knowledge transfer required to address relevant business challenges.

BP's app-based curated digital content on leadership development is delivered in a bite-sized format consisting of interactive infosheets, various leadership scenarios with real-world vignettes and short summaries of common leadership mistakes, all of which are tailored to emerging business needs. This allows mid-level executives to gain quick take-aways and application opportunities to enhance generic leadership capabilities within a contextualised business environment. However, this content is more targeted towards emerging and mid-level managers and is therefore unsuitable for more senior level executives responsible for addressing more challenging business-related issues involving complex business model innovation and may benefit more from other development interventions discussed in Chapter 2.

Another key benefit of this app is that it allows BP to automate and continuously compare employee feedback on managers performance across a range of capabilities which are then compared against the average score of peers across the business as well as enabling managers to adjust their behaviours to suite the motivational factors of their team.[32]

Even where bespoke content is created specifically for executives in an organisation, it may still not address specific individual needs and the context of challenges faced by executives in one division may differ from others and therefore other forms of intervention such as coaching, mentoring or other experiential learning modalities may be more suitable for addressing development needs. Hence, curated content should be employed as an augmentation or reinforcement mechanism to support other development modalities, such as podcast to reinforce coaching techniques, or videos on digital strategy development to support an experiential learning assignment in rolling out new digital business models.

Breadth of complementary development offerings: owing to greater financial capacity larger organisations can have access to a wide range of executive development offerings and can dovetail in curated and other digital learning technologies as an augmentation to other development modalities. On the other hand, smaller organisations constrained by cost pressures are more likely to rely on curated content to deliver executive development and can augment this with other cost-effective experiential approaches such as serving on boards of charitable organisations and other modalities discussed in previous sections of this chapter.

Summary of key points

This chapter has addressed the organisational size considerations, learning needs assessment process for executives, including how executive development can be tailored to address organisational culture climate challenges, sector dynamics and how appropriate digital technology and platforms can be effectively integrated into the learning architecture

The size of an organisation is a crucial factor in determining the scale and scope of the executive development interventions required to drive value and long-term growth.

Some of the challenges that large organisations are likely to face which can be addressed through effective executive development include; Slow responsiveness in changing the organisational value systems and structure; Presence of counterproductive sub-cultures which can hinder innovation and creativity; Capital adequacy overconfidence, resulting in investment in non-value adding ventures, Differential performance across divisions, geographic location and business units; Over-reliance of debt financing and mergers to rapidly expand business with limited value creation; Decline in risk appetite, experimentation and risk-taking behaviour to drive the innovation and creativity across all divisions; Limited interdepartmental cooperation and silo mentality hindering innovation, creativity; Decision ineffectiveness and delays in strategy implementation.

Small and medium sized firms tend to be less prone to some of the structural drag which stifles creativity and innovation but face other unique challenges which need to be reflected in the design of executive development programmes such as: Limited funds and resource constraints resulting in delayed product launch; Growth Challenges (fast versus slow); Developing the company culture during expansion into other markets; Groupthink owing to relatively small executive cohort which can result in ineffective decision making; Organisational design during expansion and to maximise disruption; Market selection, speed of penetration and optimising the impact of these actions on financial position.

The impact of megatrends such as automation and machine learning is likely to disrupt certain industries and sectors much faster than others so the speed of learning and repositioning of business models will need to be accelerated to match.

Variabilities in the maturity levels of executive development across sectors have been observed which has implications on the deployment of the design and implementation of executive development. This calls for executive development in the underperforming sectors to take a more engaging and nurturing approach as per discussions in Chapter 3 for less matured organisations.

By deploying specific executive development interventions, the prevailing culture can be influenced by executives to enable them set appropriate values and behavioural models which can be reinforced through acceptance and replication by other leaders and then eventually become embedded across board. Some of the key organisational challenges which can be addressed through executive development include; culture lagging with customer experience, incongruence of sub-cultures, cross-cultural and diversity misalignment, and breaking down of hierarchical cultures.

Effectively executive development is crucial for building the business case for the development programme, and for determining the best modalities to adopt for both individual and team executives, including aggregation of delivery modalities to achieve economies of scale (organisational size permitting).

Executive development gap analysis processes should take into account the current and future value and growth drivers, industry level challenges and positioning of competitors along the value chain. Consideration should also be given to mapping of any threat of emerging disruptors and innovators across the value chain, including any emerging megatrends, customer trends, internal operational deficiencies, and regulatory changes that will impact on the ability of the organisation to achieve its growth targets.

The 5-As (Awareness, Acceptance, Action/Application, Assessment & Affirmation) development model can be employed to map out clear steps for developing individual executives' capabilities.

The important link between identification of individual capabilities gaps and that of the team is predicated on building a culture of openness, honesty and self-awareness which can create a conducive environment for individuals to feel more comfortable about discussing their own development needs.

Digital platforms can be employed to provide synchronous and asynchronous, just-in-time and micro learning to address capability gaps in technological developments in AI, deep learning, machine learning, virtual reality, and other emerging areas of digital technology, which can be fitted around the work patterns of busy executives, providing bite-sized learning which is easily digestible and can be applied to real-time challenges.

References

1. Harvard Business Publishing, *The State of Leadership Development* (Harvard Business Publishing 2016) https://www.harvardbusiness.org/sites/default/files/19770_CL_StateOfLeadership_Report_July2016.pdf (last accessed 21 January 2018).
2. Rick Mullin, 'Tufts study finds big rise in cost of drug development – pharmaceuticals: benchmark report sees the cost of bringing a drug to market approaching $3 billion' (*C&EN* 20 November 2017) https://cen.acs.org/articles/92/web/2014/11/Tufts-Study-Finds-Big-Rise.html (last accessed 21 January 2018).
3. Russell Reynolds Associates, 'Insights into hr future of the top pharma boards' (Russell Reynolds Associates 2016) http://www.russellreynolds.com/en/Insights/thought-leadership/Documents/Insights%20into%20the%20future%20of%20top%20pharma%20boards_RRA_Jun%202016_online.pdf (last accessed 22 January 2018).
4. Boyden, 'Executive Monitor: Energy Mining & Industry' (*Boyden Insights* 2015) https://www.boyden.com/media/energy-mining-and-industrials-169895/index.html (last accessed 22 January 2018).
5. Cecilia Jamasmie, 'Tanzania-focused miners face fresh challenges as country passes new laws' (Mining.com 4| July 2017) http://www.mining.com/tanzania-focused-miners-face-fresh-challenges-as-country-passes-new-laws/ (last accessed 22 January 2018).

6. Asha McLean, 'Rio Tinto preparing for the Mine of the Future with automation' (*Zdnet* 26 February 2018) https://www.zdnet.com/article/rio-tinto-preparing-for-the-mine-of-the-future-with-automation/ (last accessed 28 February 2018).

7. Michelle Ash, 'At Barrick, innovation is everyone's business' (*Barrick Gold* 28 February 2017) http://barrickbeyondborders.com/mining/2017/02/innovation-is-everyone-business/ (last accessed 20 February 2018).

8. Molly Lempriere, 'Hacking the mining industry' (Mining Technology 21 November 2016) https://www.mining-technology.com/features/featurehacking-the-mining-industry-5674856/ (last accessed 20 February 2018).

9. Amy Shuen, Paul F. Feiler and David J. Teece, 'Dynamic capabilities in the upstream oil and gas sector: Managing next generation competition' (2014) 3 *Energy Strategy Reviews* 5.

10. Anoop Srivastava, 'Artificial Intelligence: The future of oil and gas' (*The Digitalist Magazine* 7 August 2017) http://www.digitalistmag.com/digital-supply-networks/2017/08/07/artificial-intelligence-future-of-oil-gas-05259467 (last accessed 24 January 2018).

11. Ian Turner and Dana Bernstein, 'Creating a team of Special Forces – an interview with Statoil (Duke Corporate Education September 2014) http://www.dukece.com/insights/creating-a-team-of-special-forces-an-interview-with-statoil/ (last accessed 24 January 2018).

12. Tom Baker, David Gee, Christopher Millican and Lee Pearson, 'Rewiring utilities for the power market of the future' (*BCG* 6 October 2016) https://www.bcg.com/en-gb/publications/2016/energy-environment-rewiring-utilities-power-market-future.aspx (last accessed 24 January 2018).

13. Microsoft Inc., 'Innovative utility deploys smart streetlights as digital service stations for the city of the future' (Microsoft Inc, Customer Stories 17 August 2016) https://customers.microsoft.com/en-us/story/innovative-utility-deploys-smart-streetlights-as-digital-service-stations-for-the-city-of-the-future (last accessed 24 January 2018).

14. Marilyn Waite, 'Why US utilities should invest in innovation' (Utility Dive 24 April 2017) https://www.utilitydive.com/news/why-us-utilities-should-invest-in-innovation/441114/ (last accessed 24 January 2018).

15. Dale Buss, 'Public Utility Company Exelon Shows Other Sectors and Firms How to Be Innovative' (Chief Executive, 20 August 2015) https://chiefexecutive.net/public-utility-company-exelon-shows-other-sectors-and-firms-how-to-be-innovative/ (last accessed 24 January 2018).

16. Garrett Hering, '12 disruptive innovators in the energy business' (*Green Biz* 7 July 2014) https://www.greenbiz.com/blog/2014/07/07/12-disruptive-innovators-energy-business (last accessed 25 January 2018).

17. Dayana Nevo, 'Are you ready to take the omni-channel experience to the max?' (Amdocs, 10 January 2017) https://www.amdocs.com/blog/place-digital-talks-intelligent-minds/digital_experience-are-you-ready-take-omni-channel-experience-max (last accessed 25 January 2018).

18. Levi Phillips, 'Research Shows Retailers Are Wedded to Formal Learning at Expense of Embracing Modern Learning Practices' (Towards Maturity 25 May 2016) https://towardsmaturity.org/2016/05/25/press-research-shows-retailers-wedded-formal-learning-expense-embracing-modern-learning-practices/ (last accessed 3 January 2018).

19. Caroline Igoki Mwangi, 'Emotional Intelligence Influence on Employee Engagement Sustainability in Kenyan Public Universities' (2014) 1 *International Journal of Academic Research in Public Policy and Governance* 75.

20. Genos International, 'Increasing employee engagement and leadership emotional intelligence with IBM' (Genos International Case Study) http://emotional intelligencegroup.co.uk/emotional-intelligence-case-studies/increasing-employee-engagement-and-leaders-emotional-intelligence-with-ibm/ (last accessed 3 January 2018).

21. Fran Roberts, 'Bad managers are driving talented staff away from the construction sector' (Construction Global 23 January 2018) http://www.constructionglobal.com/major-projects/bad-managers-are-driving-talented-staff-away-construction-sector (last accessed 30 January 2018).

22. Fastbrick Robotics (Fastbrick Robotics Corporate website) https://www.fbr.com.au/ (last accessed 30 January 2018).

23. Icon Build (Icon Build Corporate website) https://www.iconbuild.com/ (last accessed 30 January 2018).

24. Kip Kelly and Allan Schaefer, 'Creating a collaborative organizational culture' (UNC Executive Development 2015) http://www.kenan-flagler.unc.edu/~/media/Files/documents/executive-development/unc-white-paper-creating-a-collaborative-organizational-culture.pdf (last accessed 28 January 2018).

25. John B. McGuire, Charles J. Palus, William Pasmore, and Gary B. Rhodes, 'Transforming your organization' (Centre for Creative Leadership 2015) https://www.ccl.org/wp-content/uploads/2015/04/TYO.pdf (last accessed 28 January 2018).

26. A. Y. Kolb and D. A. Kolb, 'Learning styles and learning spaces: Enhancing experiential learning in higher education' (2005) 4 *Academy of Management Learning & Education* 193–212.

27. Ray I. Chang, Yu Hsin Hung and Chun Fu Lin, 'Survey of learning experiences and influence of learning style preferences on user intentions regarding MOOCs' (2015) 46(3) *British Journal of Educational Technology* 528.

28. Sean Gallagher, 'As Corporate World Moves Toward Curated 'Microlearning,' Higher Ed Must Adapt' (*EdSurge* 6 November 2017) https://www.edsurge.com/news/2017-11-06-as-corporate-world-moves-toward-curated-microlearning-higher-ed-must-adapt (last accessed 28 January 2018).

29. IEDP, 'E-learning for Executives – Do Learning Management Systems have a future in management development?' (*IEDP* Editorial 29 June 2017) https://www.iedp.com/articles/e-learning-for-executives/ (last accessed 28 January 2018).

30. Accenture, 'Accenture Working with MIT's Sloan School of Management to Enable the Next Generation of Technology Leaders' (*Accenture News* 7 January 2015) https://newsroom.accenture.com/news/accenture-working-with-mits-sloan-school-of-management-to-enable-the-next-generation-of-technology-leaders.htm (last accessed 28 January 2018).

31. Peter Hirst, 'Learning virtually everywhere: MIT Accenture Technology Executive Development Program' (MIT Sloan Executive Education 2016) https://executive.mit.edu/blog/learning-virtually-everywhere-mit-accenture-technology-executive-development-program#.Woio8Khl9PY (last accessed 31 January 2018).

32. Nigel Paine, *Building Leadership Development Programmes: Zero-cost to high-investment programmes that work* (Kogan Page 2016) 143.

5

Aligning executive development with organisational strategy

One of the key impacts of both the VUCA environment and digital disruption is the shortening of strategic planning cycles. This means that organisations frequently have to realign their strategic value drivers (such as market penetration, internationalisation/local, innovation, customer-centricity, cost reduction) and business models to ensure that the organisation remains viable and profitable in the long-term.

'Executive development should provide avenues for making strategy dynamic, help executives define distinctive and enduring positions while offering models to change strategy and evaluate new or emerging positions. Strategy provides the focus for executive development but executive development should enable strategy development to be dynamic.'[1]

As the changes driven by the VUCA environment can be either incremental, revolutionary or discontinuous, organisations have to adjust their business models to either maintain their current market position or move into a dominant stage by adjusting their strategic value drivers. Where the change is revolutionary or disruptive, executives will invariably require new capabilities within a relatively short time, to drive the adjustment in strategic drivers, including business models to match the emerging threats or opportunities.

Failure to address misalignments between executive capabilities and the short- and long-term strategic objectives can ultimately result in poor execution outcomes – eventually resulting in loss in value and growth as the lack of executive development implies that executives will rely on outdated capabilities to drive and implement new strategic imperatives. The effects of this misalignment can be colossal as competitors may capitalise on this vacuum in capabilities to capture market share. For instance, if a retailer is moving from a purely brick-and-mortar operation to embrace digital technology, a development gap will emerge as this shift prompts operational and strategic challenges which executives may not have the right capabilities to manage.

The shift within the automobile industry from fossil-powered to battery-propelled vehicles and the related autonomous driving movement requires executives of leading car manufacturers to acquire new capabilities to match the challenge mounted by Tesla – who have blazed the trail in an industry which previously had very high barriers of entry, by moving into the passenger and trucking industries simultaneously, providing autonomous driving functionality, and shifting the distribution model to directly supply to individual customers to increase profitability, instead of relying on car dealerships. Tesla is one of the first entrants into the automobile industry since Chrysler in 1922.[2] Its disruption of the automobile sector highlights that the days of stable context are long gone, replaced by an evolving context of disruptions and counter-disruptions across all sectors. This calls for executives to expand their capabilities and to create enabling environments within their organisations in order to challenge existing boundaries of innovation and creativity and to create disruptions – or to build resilience against potential disruptors.

General Motors (GM) has employed strategic acquisition as a means of reacting to Tesla's disruption by investing US$1 billion to purchase Cruise Automation, which has been kept as a subsidiary to bolster the organisation's advancement in autonomous driving. Through this acquisition, GM executives are learning from Cruise Automations to ditch daily meetings in favour of cross-departmental teleconferences, where blockers are swiftly identified and removed and results are demanded within short timescales to accelerate product development.[3]

General Motors has recognised that strategic acquisition alone is insufficient for repositioning itself to fend off the disruptions in the auto industry. Therefore, it is providing development interventions for senior and high-potential executives to shift the mindset of the top team towards a start-up mentality to enable the organisation to leverage its global scale and footprint to address the challenges of disruptive competitors. Participants of these programmes which cut across a wider spectrum – from seasoned VPs to younger executives selected from different geographic regions and business functions – are divided into five teams to develop solutions to real business challenges, engage in interaction with start-up companies and entrepreneurs, and explore avenues to realign business cultures, values and expand their analytical thinking capabilities to drive effective decision-making.[4]

Similarly, automaker Daimler is providing development interventions for its leadership team – which includes interactions with customers and partners – to enable them systematically digitising the entire value chain encompassing methods used in the design, development and production of vehicles, to better position itself to benefit from the emerging digital economy.[5]

The predicted surge in the electric car market and its potential impact on revenue streams from fossil powered vehicles, has prompted oil major, Royal Dutch Shell to diversify from its traditional oil business model by partnering with Ionity – a joint venture between Daimler, Volkswagen Group, Ford, Porsche and Audi – to create a network of chargers across major highways in Europe.[6] This will generate revenue to off-set the projected decline in oil demand in the future. This is a new frontier for the business and will require executives involved in this venture to develop capabilities in managing the complex legal structures and the long-term relationship with multiple partners to maximise benefits.

The intensity of external pressures on organisational business models will increase significantly within this era of digital technology and will compel executives to proactively identify any capabilities gaps required to transition seamlessly from traditional to digital business models. GE, for example, has mapped out its strategic approach to transition toward a digital business model and broaden its services business model by providing its executive and leadership team with awareness of the capabilities required to deliver long-term value in the digital economy – such as artificial intelligence, user experience design, and deep machine learning – which are not common in traditional industrial firms.[7]

Recognising that the Six Sigma approach was no longer suitable for the new strategic direction, GE switched to the 'FastWorks' methodology by providing training to senior leaders to ingrain Lean Start-up mind-set and culture – which included embedding capabilities to gaining feedback from customers at an early stage of product innovation to gauge whether money was being spend in the right way.[8]

There is a high propensity for organisations to inadvertently negate the need to evaluate the executive capabilities required to successfully implement a strategic shift, and instead place more emphasis on speed of execution in the quest to leapfrog competitors with new products and service offerings. Thus, organisations assume that executives can succeed in a shifting strategic landscape with the same capabilities and often have to backtrack when they realise the gap mid execution stage and then have to resort to engaging specialist consultants and interim executives at exorbitant costs. Even when external resources are brought in, the execution of new strategic drivers can be hindered by the timescales required to recruit external candidates, which may lead to further delays in delivering the intended new business model required to fend off the competitive threats of incumbent and emerging disruptive industry players.

Whilst strategy is normally positioned as a dynamic process which provides executives with the imperative to evaluate new and emerging positions to generate solutions that can propel the organisation to grow or maintain a dominant market position, strategic initiatives can often be pursued without due recognition of the capabilities that are required for the effective implementation at both top level and other tiers within the organisational hierarchy.

Ensuring that executives have the right capabilities to drive a new strategic focus can enhance both execution speed and effectiveness. IBM transformed itself from a 'pure technology provider' to a 'high value' service provider by introducing a new breed of leaders, embedding a consulting mindset and driving a different type of innovation and creativity across the management and executive team.[9]

High-performing service organisations like Accenture and IBM align executive and leadership development programmes with strategic development at all levels to drive value generation in the short term and to position themselves to benefit from future changes in their sectors.

At Airbus, C-suite learning and development is considered to be a significant contributor to the achievement of organisations imperatives and therefore these initiatives are always tightly aligned with the current corporate strategy.[10]

Comcast Cable has also established a top-level advisory board called the National Executive Learning Council, which drives learning that is strategically aligned with business long-term objectives.[11]

Whilst these exemplar organisations proactively align strategy with executive learning, this may not be a common practice across other companies owing to sheer neglect or the pressure to deliver new strategic imperatives within short timescale and even where organisations follow this process, it's unclear how often they realign their executive development when there is change in strategic direction.

To increase the successful realignment of strategic value drivers (such as innovation, customer or cost focus) there is an imperative to assess the readiness of executives to implement these initiatives successfully to achieve the intended growth (refer to figure 5.1). Depending on the scale of the change,

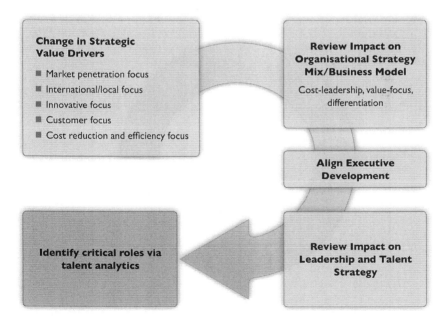

Figure 5.1 Alignment of executive development to strategic value drivers.

executive development programmes may have to be completely revamped or realigned at the individual and collective executive team level to ensure successful implementation of the intended change in strategic direction. Organisations seeking to grow through intensive M&A activities can for example make significant changes to their existing executive development programmes to account for deal origination, decision-making, trade-off analysis, post-merger-integration, legal and tax complications – all of which can minimise the dilutive effects of unsuccessful M&A activities on organisational growth.

Similarly, when the focus is on market penetration or internationalisation, executives need to gain new capabilities which will enable them to identify which markets offer the best prospects for existing products, find faster routes to market, drive competitors out of mature markets with aggressive pricing and promotional campaigns, and tap into cultural sensitivities to add new features to existing products. Another important capability that is beneficial to executives when pursuing an internationalisation strategy is learning how to select and develop local channel partners; extending and pruning them as appropriate and, using sophisticated incentives and contractual structures, to motivate high-performing channel partners given that in some countries using resellers or channel partners can achieve faster success and penetration than relying on direct sales models.[12] Where the emphasis is to broaden the appeal of existing products to a particular local market, then executives will need to develop the capabilities to position the organisation to provide enhanced customer experience, personalised offerings and disruptive products that can appeal to particular sub-cultures and values of the target market.

Invariably, the changes in the strategic drivers may require executives to develop entirely different or sometimes complementary capabilities. For instance, some of the capabilities that executives may require for innovative focus – such as creative problem-solving and risk-taking techniques – can assist in driving customer-centricity and lower cost. Whereas the capabilities required for delivering lower cost may not be complementary with market penetration if this requires high discounting in a matured market. In case an organisation turns its attention to cost-reduction as a strategic focus, executives will need to develop more insight to determine the critical cost components and factors which impact on customer experience, touch-points and value-creation by market segment and geography. Executives must also augment this insight by galvanising organisation-wide support for the shift to the cost reduction environments by demonstrating behaviours congruent with cost reduction, evaluating and terminating non-value adding investments swiftly, and agreeing the business priorities and allocating resources to activities that drive long-term value.

Where an organisation is seeking to realign multiple strategic value drivers, care must be taken not to overload executives with numerous development interventions owing to the busy lifestyles and the attention deficiency challenges that are likely to emerge, which had been mentioned in Chapter 2. Overloading executives with multiple development initiatives is likely to be counter-productive and will dilute the intended impact of the development intervention.

In case of organisations seeking to increase market penetration through a strategic alliance, consideration should be given to whether executives have the capabilities to manage any relationships challenges, deal with intellectual property issues, as well as any critical expertise required to maximise the benefits of an alliance partnership. Similarly, organisations seeking to replicate the success of platform-based models such as Lyft, Uber, Alibaba and Airbnb should consider closing any executive capabilities gaps related to understanding the complexities of various revenue models, customer preferences, as well as any legal and international labour issues which can impact on generating profit from this model. Executives' underestimation of the value drivers, operational challenges and competitive landscape is considered to be the main source of failure of platform models.[13]

Burberry, Daimler, GE, Siemens, Nike, and other organisations across different industry sectors are adopting the platform approach to create disruptive business models following the steps of other organisations that have successful implemented this model as a core business strategy (Uber, Amazon, Alibaba and Airbnb) and those who have adapted this model as an add-on (Microsoft and Apple). These successful platform disruptors have tapped into changing customer behaviours, demographics and reliability and penetration of technology such as: access to low cost shared infrastructure (cloud-based storage), greater mobile penetration rates, enhanced internet network access, to displace high cost entry barriers within some existing industries. For example, YouTube, Spotify, Amazon, Alibaba and eBay have successfully removed the entry barriers within the media, entertainment and retail sectors by launching user-driven content and just-in-time purchase decisions. Similarly within the hospitality sector, firms such as JustEat and OpenTable have aggregated unconnected and unaffiliated restaurants into a viable business model to challenge the traditional isolated and fragmented sector. Others such as RedBus and Airbnb are unlocking new value from spare resources and by amalgamating fragmented bus schedules and reshaping the urban travel business and renting models thus providing a compelling case for both existing businesses and emerging disrupters to explore any untapped opportunities to launch new platform business models.

Another important strand in the process of aligning executive development with changes in strategic direction involves identifying critical resources at the operational and management levels. Talent analytics can be employed to rapidly unearth any organisational wide gaps in the capabilities required for successful delivery of any strategic response to environmental threats. Major oil and gas companies with large-scale global footprints can utilise talent analytics to determine the profile of staff required to rebalance their operations owing to stagnant oil prices and the challenges emerging from the shift to battery powered-cars. Identification and retention of staff with complementary capabilities of any industries that such oil majors want to move into as a means of rebalancing their operations will be beneficial as existing staff who understand organisational value drivers will be better placed to lead initiatives than employing outsiders who may not be unfamiliar with existing organisational norms. Retaining and transferring existing employees into new ventures can result in a 'critical mass' to transfer and embed organisational core values and mindsets to new staff recruited to help deliver these initiatives. This approach can help speed up the effective execution of new strategic initiatives. Executives in organisations facing similar challenges will need to enhance their capabilities to identify and map out the key talent metrics which are likely to have the greatest impact on the successful delivery of new strategic initiatives. This will allow them to map any existing talent with complementary capabilities required in a new business model before any downsizing can occur.

Transitioning from an old to new business model can lead to the loss of key customers that may be impacted by the mismanagement of unforeseen challenges. Therefore, executives need to develop the capabilities necessary to ensure a flawless transition, in terms of managing the expectations and communications to high-value customers, and formulation of robust mitigation strategies to address operational pinch-points to ensure successful delivery of new strategic initiates/business model without impacting the delivery of services to existing customers. Organisations will invariably embark on numerous waves of strategic change initiatives which may have a significant operational impact, and this will warrant the need for conducting executive development needs analysis (refer to Chapter 4 for more details about this process), which should be integral to the strategy formulation and implementation phases. By building learning needs analysis into the formulation/review of strategy, organisations can enhance their capacity to minimise the impact of operational bottlenecks, achieve quick wins, accelerate time-to-market durations and leapfrog competitors to create value and growth. By frequently realigning executive development interventions to reflect changes in strategic direction – especially where this involves a step change in the business model or strategic direction – organisations will significantly increase their chances of execution success by allocating sufficient time to plan, deliver and embed new capabilities for executives and critical employees thereby improving the chances of successful execution.

The action-process-impact (output) approach which offers a useful framework to align strategic value drivers with executive development to ensure sustainable growth and value generation in organisations is summarised in table 5.1 with an expansion of each step provided below.

Review strategic value drivers: The review of strategic value drivers can help to unearth new/obsolete ones, including any barriers to growth as well as risks to successful strategy execution that can limit the capacity of the organisation to grow organically or through business combinations. This will invariably result in the identification of new value drivers and new business models suitable for short- and long-term value generation and growth.

Align corporate strategies to business models: Once strategic value drivers are established, executives need to align them with new business model (s) as well as the overarching corporate strategy and, where necessary, carve out a completely new strategy if the existing one no longer fits long-term organisational objectives.

The executive team will need to validate the congruence of existing and new business models in order to develop a coherent corporate strategy that aligns fully with the value and growth trajectory of the organisation, as well as considering the critical resources required for the successful execution of the revised strategy.

This step will also involve mapping out the individual and executive team input to the delivery of the new business model, including identification of any overlapping responsibilities, cross-functional structures and the metrics for evaluation the successful implementation of the new business model.

The outcome at this stage will be in the form of a revised strategic plan with a robust execution plan; trade-off options, prioritisation of initiatives, mitigation plans, operational targets and key delivery milestones.

Establish specific and cross-functional executive input required to execute strategy: Next, specific and cross-functional executive input required to execute strategy will be obtained to secure the buy-in at the top-level to ensure that each individual executive is supportive of the new direction pursued by the organisation and the opportunity for identifying any capability gaps required to drive the new business model. The current capabilities of executives can be compared against the capabilities required to drive the new business model or strategic direction. During this process, executives must be transparent, vulnerable, comfortable and be willing to admit any deficiencies in the capabilities required to drive the new strategic direction. Any diagnostic capability evaluation tools used to evaluate the gaps across the executive team should be supplemented by team coaching to address any group-think and biases which can influence the robustness of the evaluation. The outcome of this process should be a review of individual and executive team capability frameworks juxtaposed against the present and future business models and strategy direction of the organisation.

Conduct executive capabilities gap analysis: This will prepare the grounds for conducting detailed capabilities gap analysis within the executive team, exploring any cognitive, emotional and intellectual capabilities as well as the relevant value driving capabilities discussed in Chapter 2. The gap analysis should be conducted at the individual and team levels and should explore the specific knowledge, skills, personal characteristics and demonstrable behaviours required to deliver the new strategy. It should also consider an assessment of all executives (and all those identified as highest potential) to identify those who have the desired competencies. More importantly, at this stage, the executive team need to differentiate between strategic value-adding and non-value-adding capabilities so that time and useful resources are not expended on developing any set of non-value-adding capabilities. The outcome of this stage should include;

a) Detailed assessment of specific individual /collective executive readiness and creation of initial capability models for future utilisation.
b) Modification of existing capability models or creation of new profile specific to align with the new strategic direction/model whilst provisioning for future-centricity.
c) Identification of the strategic/critical roles required for the successful implementation of the new strategy at the department/cross-functional/ business unit/ levels, including consideration of ecosystem participation and specialist expertise required from outside parties.
d) Executive Committee and/or appropriate board committee validation of new capabilities models across all levels (including executives) vis-à-vis future requirements and instigation of detailed action plans.

Table 5.1 Alignment of strategic value drivers with executive development

Action	Process	Impact/Output
1. Review strategic value drivers	Identify the new value drivers, barriers and risks to strategy execution and impact on operations.	**Establish new strategic value drivers /new business models which account for short- and long-term value generation and growth.**
2. Align corporate strategies to business models	Develop a corporate strategy that aligns fully with the business model, taking into account resources required for successful execution of the strategy.	**Revised strategy with a robust execution plan; prioritisation of initiatives, mitigation plans for barriers, operational targets and key milestones.**
3. Establish specific and cross-functional executive input required to execute strategy	Establish input of business units and departments taking into account ongoing initiatives versus identified future initiatives required to deliver new business model and strategy.	**Individual and executive team capability frameworks addressing present and future business model and strategy requirements.**
4. Conduct executive capabilities gap analysis	Individual assignment and development.	**Assess specific individual readiness and create plans for future utilisation.**

Action	Process	Impact/Output
	Model of the specific knowledge, skills, personal characteristics and demonstrable behaviours required to deliver the strategy.	**Adapt existing competency model or create new one specific to strategy and build in an element of future centricity.**
	Assessment of all executives (and all those identified as highest potential) to identify those who have the desired competencies.	**Committee and/or appropriate board committee reviews executives vis-à-vis future requirements and instigates action plan.**
	Differentiating between strategic value-adding and non-value-adding capabilities.	**Narrowing the focus to the roles that are strategic and identifying the most critical roles that implement strategy or support strategic roles.**
5. Assess HR systems and processes to support executive development	Support, create or modify HR systems such as compensation, performance management, executive development, recruiting and out-placement to perform step 7 and to manage performance of strategic executives.	**Revised compensation and performance management plans, mapping of new executive roles to strategic initiatives, revised recruitment and on-boarding strategies.**
6. Talent and leadership gap analysis (Lower tier executive level)	Map out the leadership and talent gaps at 3–4 levels below top executives across the organisation required to drive the new strategy.	**Revised talent management grid maps and robust implementation plan to support delivery of new strategy at the operational and tactical levels.**
7. Executive capability acquisition and development	Implement specific individual / team development plans to acquire desired capabilities.	**Implementation of development plans, assess effectiveness and speed of delivery, evaluation mechanisms, and lessons learnt.**
8. Ongoing review and re-alignment	**Conduct ongoing review and re-alignment of value drivers, strategy and executive development.**	**Implement minor or major changes to executive development as dictated by market conditions and shifts in business model and strategy.**

Assess HR systems and processes to support executive development: A detailed assessment and review of existing HR processes and systems is vital to ensure that executives are not only motivated to engage in a new development intervention required to deliver new strategic initiatives but, more importantly, that adequate metrics can be developed to monitor and evaluate the effectiveness of the development interventions that will be deployed as a result of the revised strategic direction of the organisation. Some of the key outputs of this step will include a revised compensation and performance management plan, revised recruitment and on-boarding strategies and mapping of new executive roles to drive the strategic initiatives, depending on the scale of the strategic change. Where there is a significant shift in strategy then a far-reaching change in the HR system beyond the executive level to other lower tier executives needs to be considered during this stage of the process.

Talent and leadership gap analysis (lower tier executive level): Given the significant contribution that lower tier executives offer to the successful implementation of strategic initiatives (which was discussed in chapter 1), it is critical to map out the leadership and talent gaps at three or four levels below the top executives across the organisation. This process can be expedited by using HR data analytics to map out relevant employees. Once gaps are identified, the scale and complexity of development needs required to drive the new strategic direction can be determined, including consideration of how quickly these capability gaps can be filled and which development modalities can most effectively be deployed without disruption to existing strategic, operational and tactical targets. The outputs from this stage will include revised talent management grid maps and a robust implementation plan to support the effective delivery of new strategy at the operational and tactical levels which can be monitored. An assessment of the prevailing culture and readiness for change will also be beneficial to ensure that adequate provision can be made in the design of development interventions to drive an organisational culture which supports the new strategy direction of the organisation.

Executive capability development: The organisation's readiness to proceed with the new strategy needs to be solidified by rolling out specific individual and team development plans to close any identified capability gaps. The implementation of these development interventions should be monitored, measured by the CEO and the board to ensure accountability, and any identified misalignment with the strategy should be addressed. Each individual executive member should be accountable for their own and team development plans up to three or four tiers below the c-suite, supported by clear metrics demonstrating how the outcomes of the development is enabling the successful implementation of the strategy. Organisations may understand the steps required to move into a new strategic direction, but too often they underestimate the level of effort required to underpin this with a congruent culture and the impact of a dysfunctional culture in destroying value across all levels including product, channel, geography, market segment or business unit. And few ultimately understand the cascading effect this impact can have across the entire organisation.

Ongoing review and realignment: Executive development effectiveness should be integral to regular strategic business reviews. This will allow adjustments to modalities of development interventions, test their relevance to current value drivers and strategy direction of the organisation. This review can be an opportunity to assess capabilities across the executive bench in terms of readiness to implement any emerging strategic initiatives or drive potential disruptions. The outcome of this exercise will be in the form of minor or major changes to the executive development modalities which will be dictated by market conditions or any shifts in business models and organisational strategy. For example, if the review prompts a shift towards greater ecosystem relationships, then development interventions should be designed to enhance the collaborative capabilities of executives and a cultural alignment within strategic divisions interfacing with ecosystem partners.

By following the above steps, organisations will be not only be well prepared to deliver new strategic initiatives but this will prompt executives continually to enhance their own capabilities, as well as those of the employees within their immediate span of control, to launch disruptive business models successfully in order to drive long-term value and growth.

Summary of key points

The realignment of strategic drivers owing to environmental threats and business model disruptions is becoming a more frequent feature in organisations. But in addressing this situation, organisations may fail to conduct a capability audit of their executive cohort to ensure that they are well equipped to drive any new strategic agenda, and they may resort to either employing consultants or bringing on board interims at a much higher cost with potential delays to implementation.

Attention needs to be given to mapping out the capabilities required for the new strategic direction so that adequate development interventions can be implemented to ensure that executives are well prepared to deliver new business models in a successful and timely manner. This approach helps to maximise the value that can be generated from strategic initiatives implemented to respond to environmental threats, by ensuring that executives are well prepared to deliver and embed any emerging strategic initiatives ahead of competitors.

An action, process, impact model with clear steps for embedding executive cohort capability is a useful way of ensuring a seamless approach to responding to the occasional realignment of strategic direction and delivering emerging business model needs prompted by the VUCA environment and disruptive competitors.

References

1. Richard Thorpe, *Gower Handbook of Leadership and Management Development* (CRC, 5th edn, 2016) 107.
2. Brent Goldfarb, 'Why Tesla is overhyped — and overvalued - Tesla and the deep problems with "disruption" theory' (*Vox,* 1 August 2017) < https://www.vox.com/the-big-idea/2017/6/26/15872468/tesla-gm-ford-valuation-justifying-disruption > accessed 20 November 2017.
3. Erin Griffith, 'Driven in the Valley: The Startup Founders Fueling GM's Future' (*Fortune* 22 September 2016) < http://fortune.com/cruise-automation-general-motors-driverless-cars/ > accessed 23 November 2017.
4. Melissa Burden, 'GM works with Stanford to train execs, change culture' (*Detroit News* 17 February 2016) <https://www.detroitnews.com/story/business/autos/general-motors/2016/02/17/gm-works-stanford-train-execs-change-culture/80530328/> accessed 23 November 2017.
5. Daimler, *Our Strategy,* (Daimler 2018) <https://www.daimler.com/company/strategy/ > accessed 13 March 2018.
6. Rakteem Katakey, 'Shell Joins Automakers to Offer Charging Stations Across Europe' (*Bloomberg,* 27 November 2017) < https://www.bloomberg.com/news/articles/2017-11-27/shell-joins-automakers-to-offer-charging-stations-across-europe > accessed 30 December 2017.
7. Art Kleiner and John Sviokla, 'The Thought Leader Interview: GE's Bill Ruh on the Industrial Internet Revolution' (*Strategy + business,* issue 86 1 February 2017) < https://www.strategy-business.com/article/The-Thought-Leader-Interview-Bill-Ruh?gko=9ae51 > accessed 30 December 2017.
8. Brad Power, 'How GE Applies Lean Startup Practices' (*HBR* 23 April 2014) < https://hbr.org/2014/04/how-ge-applies-lean-startup-practices > accessed 30 December 2017.
9. Richard L. Nolan, *Executive Team Leadership in the Global Economic and Competitive Environment* (Routledge, 2014) 106.
10. Daniel Chadwick, 'The CLO in the C-Suite: how can learning get heard? - Aligning learning and leadership development with corporate strategy' (IEDP 26 November 2015) < http://www.iedp.com/articles/the-clo-in-the-c-suite-how-can-learning-get-heard/> accessed 30 December 2017.
11. Kathy Caprino, 'The Top 7 Secret Confessions From The C-Suite About Talent Development' (*Forbes* 5 June 2016) < https://www.forbes.com/sites/kathycaprino/2016/06/05/the-top-7-secret-confessions-from-the-c-suite-about-talent-development/#28af52001174> accessed 30 December 2017.
12. Nataly Kelly, 'The Most Common Mistakes Companies Make with Global Marketing' (*HBR* 7 September 2015) < https://hbr.org/2015/09/the-most-common-mistakes-companies-make-with-global-marketing > accessed 30 December 2017.
13. Marshall W. Van Alstyne, Geoffrey G. Parker, and Sangeet Paul Choudary, 'Reasons why platforms fail' (*HBR* 31 March 2016) < https://hbr.org/2016/03/6-reasons-platforms-fail > accessed 30 December 2017.

6

Bridging the gap between executive development and organisational performance

At the heart of the concept of creating value and growth through executive development is the view that executive development programmes must be aligned with the firm's organisational architecture (structure, systems, technology, culture and values) and strategic initiatives. This theme, which was explored briefly in Chapter 1, is expanded upon in this chapter.

Investing in executive development programmes and expecting this investment to automatically result in value creation and growth is a very easy trap for organisations to fall into, given that the impact of executive development on organisational growth does not occur in a vacuum. Further action is required to align the organisational architecture to create an enabling environment which can facilitate the effective implementation of strategic initiatives. Failure to align the organisational architecture impedes the transfer of dynamic capabilities from the executive team through the leadership structure to the front-line staff who are responsible for delivering strategic initiatives necessary for creating value and growth. Some organisations well known for implementing effective executive development programmes have become victims of incongruence between executive development programmes and organisational architecture. Procter and Gamble (P&G), for example, has consistently been featured as an exceptional organisation in terms of developing executives and leaders but its performance has lagged behind key competitors such as Unilever and Colgate-Palmolive, even though both competitors of P&G have had a perceived lower ranking in terms of developing leadership capabilities.

P&G is also losing market share in some of its core markets to competitors. For example, Ontex – which is a small Belgian company which has gone through rapid growth within a short time – has expanded to Mexico, which is traditionally a core market for P&G.[2]

For a number of years, the performance of competitors such as Unilever and Johnson & Johnson has exceeded that of P&G, although in recent times P&G is making improvements following simplifying of its structure to create a more focused, agile and more accountable organisation to improve innovation and productivity across it portfolio of products.[1]

The example of P&G highlights that investing in executive development programmes without realignment of the organisational architecture at the strategic, tactical and operational levels can impede the translation of executive development outcomes to drive value and growth. Executive development programmes should not only equip participants with the capacity to provide an enabling environment to innovate and challenge the norms for growth, but also confer the capabilities to realign the organisational architecture to maximise the outcomes of executive development. This step can be the most challenging phase of the journey to drive value and growth through executive development initiatives because these components of organisational architecture often take years to form and any attempt to instigate realignment can be a painful process, although entirely necessary for creating sustainable growth.

Some of the key value-creating capabilities that executives need to leverage during this stage are summarised in table 6.1 below, so executives will need to hone these before embarking on the realignment of organisational architecture. Some of the most effective development modalities which will enable executives to succeed at this stage include: simulations (on managing complex changes and scenarios), though-leader/expert led seminars/courses on decision-making and communication effectiveness, ethical diversity management and unconsciousness bias training, deep-dive reviews, reflection exercises (prediction of possible challenging questions and scenarios and response plans), and coaching on goal achievement and effective change management.

Organisation that have the capacity to combine organic growth with other forms of business combinations and partnerships (e.g. M&A, asset swaps, alliances) can leverage executive development at the strategic level to improve M&A success rates as a vast number of M&A deals have failed to deliver the anticipated synergistic value and growth owing to the lack of alignment with value drivers and underestimation of the integration challenges (as discussed in Chapter 1). Executives can therefore develop the right capabilities to undertake effective diagnostics of deals in terms of their alignment with value drivers, and integrate them by taking into account the similarities and differences in the organisational architecture of the target candidate for the merger, acquisition, alliance, partnering or asset swap to reduce the risks of deal failure. This should include a deep-dive evaluation of the organisational architecture of all parties and the identification of any gaps so that adequate measures can be implemented to ensure that executives have the right capabilities to manage the integration and partnering challenges that will affect the combined entities' organisational architecture.

Executives need decision-making efficacy to evaluate, select and implement the most effective organisational architecture to deliver the current and projected future growth profile. This must be combined with effective change leadership necessary for championing the transformation, generating the critical mass amongst key employees and to predict/deal with any resistance that

Table 6.1 Summary of value-generating executive capabilities for re-alignment of organisational architecture

Change Leadership – Champions and drives efficient delivery of innovation and change initiatives.
Strategic Orientation - Effective implementation of strategy and clear definition of tangible steps to be taken across business units / divisions.
Decision-making - Making effective decisions to seize opportunities to drive value and growth.
Team leadership – Cross-functional collaboration and influence to drive innovation and problem solving.
Ethical and emotional intelligence – Reflection on behaviours and demonstrating and promoting ethical conduct and integrity.
Inclusiveness - Building a culture that embraces professionalism and diversity, and celebrates the uniqueness of individuals.
Results Orientation - Drive for higher performance across business units and operations.

will occur. Successful delivery of the most suitable architecture will also be dependent on executives' ability to break the strategy down into tangible steps that can be implemented across business units, focusing on results and instilling cross-functional working – without sacrificing the levels of inclusiveness, ethical conduct and integrity necessary for bonding people together during challenging transition from the old to the new paradigm.

In most cases, the realignment of the organisational architecture needs to be driven across the strategic, operational and tactical levels to facilitate the successful translation of outputs from executive development programmes to drive performance, as summarised in figure 6.1.

Strategic level: Most of the time, at the strategic level, executives – having gained the right set of capabilities through effective development programmes – are well placed to launch various change projects to drive value and growth (organically or through appropriate business combinations), depending on firm size, age and sector trends. However, having completed development programmes, executives can face a herculean task in terms of successfully implementing change projects and programmes and embedding a value and growth mind-set across the board if the organisation architecture is characterised by high inflexibility, and entrenched views of 'this is how we do things here'.

The executives must address this mind-set head-on by conducting an assessment of the main components of the organisational architecture (structure, systems, culture and values) to determine the degree of alignment with the proposed strategic initiatives which can be achieved through anonymised employee surveys/interviews /focused groups and peer reviews (at the level) with the data analysed by departmental, regional, divisional, and leadership levels to unearth any possible trends through a series of workshops facilitated by either internal or external consultants. The analysis of key trends

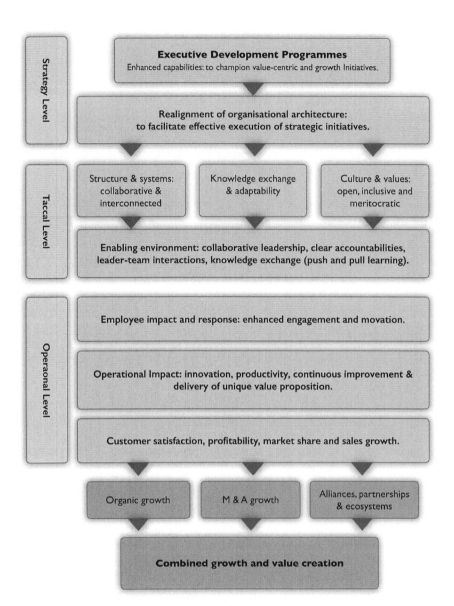

Figure 6.1 Steps for bridging the executive development and organisational performance gap.

can also be achieved with the support of data analytics or by using software packages which often have additional cost implications. Action plans must be developed to address any misalignments and monitored and reviewed continuously to ensure that an enabling climate is in place for the successful implementation of strategic initiatives at the tactical and operational levels. Cisco's collaborative leadership programme, for example, has strong board support, is connected to value-drivers, aligned to long-term strategic growth and is provided cross-functional executive involvement to drive the successful implementation of strategic initiatives carved out of executive development programmes.

Realigning the organisational architecture to facilitate effective execution of strategic initiatives must feature prominently on the board agendas so that entrenched political positions and blockers to the successful implementation can be resolved at the highest level of the organisational hierarchy. Intel, ABB and Siemens are amongst organisations that provide adequate oversight and support at the board level to review and facilitate the realignment of organisational architecture to enable effective deployment of strategic initiatives arising from executive and leadership development programmes.

The imperative for realigning the organisational structure will become more crucial owing to digitisation, automation, intensity of competition across maturing and emerging markets and the more frequent levels of disruption that will occur across all industries and sectors. To survive in the digital economy, organisations will need to become adept at orchestrating disruptions or suffer irreversible damage from disruptors.

Below is a recap of some of the avenues available to organisations in instigating digital disruptions.

Disrupt adjacent industries: Develop an entirely new business model, in an adjacent industry where it is possible to leverage existing knowledge and capabilities (e.g. Amazon to food retailing, IBM to consulting)

Disrupt in partnership with ecosystem: Create a more compelling value proposition in new markets through connections with other companies to enhance the value available to the customer to improve customer experiences, collaborate more effectively with partners, and drive ongoing innovation in products and services (such as Nike collaborating with customers, external software developers, and hardware companies to build digital fitness tracking innovation).

Disrupt current model: Creating new products, services and platforms to dilute the impact of disruptors, and leveraging inherent strengths to build the new business model (Uber to public transportation, Telsa into the automobile sector).

Aggressive digitisation: Fast-tracking the implementation of digital platforms to ensure a seamless interaction between customers in the co-creation, design, delivery of new products and to deepen the level of experience in existing product offerings.

The level of realignment of the architecture will depend on the speed of digitisation and intensity of disruption faced by the organisation. Moreover, the degree of realignment of organisational architecture will increase with the level of disruption in the following order; aggressive digitisation, disrupts in adjacent industries, partnership with ecosystem, current model (see figure 6.2).

As organisations move along the continuum of digital disruption, the challenges of cultural transformation and the degree of internal and external collaboration required across all levels of the organisation increases exponentially, and much greater effort is needed to achieve a successful outcome in terms of creating value and growth. For example, an organisation can possibly launch disruptions within its current model if there is an evolving or performing cultural transformation/internal collaboration climate but the chances of being successful at ecosystem or full-scale digitisation will be more challenging and likely to fail at this level of cultural maturity.

The success rate of digital transformation programmes is low, with only one in eight organisations likely to meet intended objectives, especially when it involves the implementation of business models requiring disruptions of the current model or aggressive digitisation across the entire business. (These models were discussed in Chapter 1.) The failure is attributed mainly to the underestimation of the expected shift in the level of interactions, behaviours, and cultural transformation required.[3]

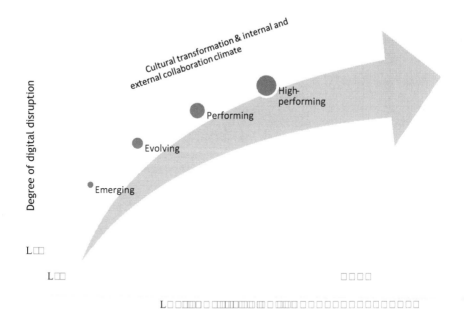

Figure 6.2 Cultural transformation implications for digital disruption against organisational architecture re-alignment.

Microsoft's approach to digital disruption combines incrementally and ecosystem partnerships with the emphasis on cultural transformation rather than focusing on technological aspects in a manner that aligns with its individual businesses to prevent an upheaval to its revenue model.[4] Such an approach may not be suitable for executives of organisations operating outside the technological space as they may face a steep learning curve in gauging the cultural challenges required to position their organisation to deliver the needs of customers in the digital economy.

To prepare employees to embrace the collaborative mindset necessary for functioning within the ecosystem working environment, organisations can adopt the fluctuating open team approach (FLOT) used in the pharma industry for drug discovery projects. This involves setting up a core internal team and providing them with the facility to tap into a diverse pool of external talent at crucial points to help accelerate decision-making and to remove obstacles in the innovation process.[5] FLOTs can serve as a soft launch /transitioning platform for employees to shift "authoritarian" behaviours before participating in ecosystem working environment - where the lines of authority can often be blurred but is a necessary climate for the ideation required for generating disruptive innovation. Executives can participate in the FLOTs process, using it as an experiential learning to deepen their understanding of the challenges encountered by employees, and to provide employees adequate support/resources for driving effective innovation.

Another useful approach to building a deeper collaboration culture and mind-set is the Microsoft mixed-reality academy model, where external developers are invited to collaborate, learn, and to accelerate the development of the reality experiences for Microsoft HoloLens and Windows Mixed Reality headsets and this has contributed towards the accelerated development of this technology.[6] Microsoft employees work with external developers at various 'Meetup', Developers' Network and User Group sessions organised across various countries, which is augmented by a number of online discussions forums to allow further development/refinements of the technology to enhance customer experience, which will maximize the value created by the product.

Another approach used by Amazon, Intel and Microsoft and Société Generale is to run hackathons (which are open innovation events where selected participants – students, coders, start-up entrepreneurs, customers, scientist, coders, educators, etc are invited to help co-create solutions to challenges faced by the organisation within a very short time, often between one and two days' duration). This can offer employees the platform to develop collaboration across disciplines and advocate for new ideas from a wider ecosystem. Hackathons with a group of start-up entrepreneurs, for example, can provide executives with the capacity to reflect on their current decision-making approaches and speed of consensus building, in order to improve their decision-making effectiveness. These events can also be used for the identification of reverse mentoring candidates for executives in the area of digital transformation.

Executives also need to invest time in developing greater levels of engagement and preparing direct reports (top-level managers two to three tiers below) to ensure successful implementation of strategic initiatives carved out from executive development programmes. These top-level managers must be given early visibility and involvement in the decision-making process pertaining to strategic initiatives, such as efficiency and cost programmes. Early engagement at this level will forge a sense of co-ownership between executives and their direct reports and solidify the foundation on which further alignment of employees can be achieved. This early engagement allows executives to gain valuable feedback to test the preparedness of the top two to three tiers of the organisational leadership structure for the execution of the change in strategic direction or new strategic initiative. Another benefit of early engagement is that it enables executives to create a critical mass quickly across the organisation so that when the strategic initiatives are formally rolled out, there is less resistance – or at least some of the possible blockers are likely to be anticipated through the early consultations and engagement with the top two to three tiers of the organisational leadership so that adequate contingency plans can be developed ahead of the implementation phase. This consultative approach needs to be extended to gauge the readiness of cross-functional support so that any potential blockers (such as incongruous sub-cultures, legacy processes, and departmental and leadership turf wars) or incompatible value systems can be resolved at the executive level. Leader–leader exchanges and peer-assisted networking events should be organised within the organisation to help break down any entrenched silo mentality that can block the implementation of change projects/programmes requiring cross-functional input. Executives should also engage with peers to identify any non-value adding projects and entrenched political ambitions (pursued to advance the career aspirations of an individual executive) that can stifle the successful implementation of new strategic initiatives and, where possible, elevate these to the board level for resolution.

Tactical level: A significant part of the action plans formulated at the strategic level will be implemented at the tactical level where most of the senior and middle managers function. Re-alignment of the of key elements of the organisational architecture is necessary to secure the engagement/commitment levels of senior and middle managers at the forefront of creating the enabling environment necessary for successful execution of value-centric initiatives across the organisation.

Organisations with a predominantly hierarchical thinking and structure (governance structure top down) must shift towards a more collaborative leadership approach across departments and divisions to shape and embed the enabling environment required for successful execution of value-centric initiatives. As the shift in leadership mind-set and culture can take considerable time to evolve, organisations need to plan well in advance to ensure that the intended cultural transformation is embedded to support any revised strategic direction.

For example, the auto-maker Daimler's quest to transform from an automobile manufacturer to a mobility service provider is hinged on establishing a collaborative team culture and a leadership mind-set which enables learning and cross-fertilisation of ideas on emerging digital innovations across its global operations, to enable the organisation to better understand and respond to the digital practices that are developing globally. This mind-set shift also includes getting to a point where some business functions and projects operate without a leadership hierarchy ensuring even more flexibility with greater shift towards agile structures.[7]

The alignment process also involves removing the hierarchical mind-set by empowering leaders across the organisations to become more accountable and goal-oriented, ensuring that all employees have visibility of how their work contributes towards the strategic goals of the organisations. Effective channels of communication also need to be opened across the organisations to allow effective transmission of knowledge from the top-level to front-line employees by providing coaching interventions that can enable executives to promote open dialogue, build stronger personal relationships and trust. Executives must also help to build and leverage internal and network through which all members of the organisation can share, nurture and develop ideas to develop new products or services.

Equally, avenues should be provided for ideas to be transmitted upwards from the front-line staff to the executive level. Further alterations to the organisational architecture to support effective implementation of value-centric/strategic initiatives are outlined below.

Structure and systems: In most cases, realigning the organisational architecture at the tactical levels involves unearthing and dismantling possible non-collaborative tendencies situated within the organisational hierarchy. Such dysfunctional cultures can institutionalise autocratic management styles which are counter-productive to the effective implementation of cross-functional projects, innovative initiatives and knowledge transfers. Where clusters, silos and turfs are identified, executive team members should work with their direct reports and across the management teams to document a collective approach to the development journey and pledge to work across board to evolve and embed a collaborative approach within the organisation. Dismantling these cultures also require executives (individually and collectively) to redefine the prevailing leadership philosophy and structure by establishing a mind-set which conditions and allows the empowerment of employees, moving from a command-and-control mind-set to a state where inclusivity, diversity and meritocracy are not held as mere tokenisms but practiced and cultivated within the organisational hierarchy. This can be achieved through coaching interventions and reflective practice to assist the executive team including other leaders (two to three tiers within the organisational hierarchy) to adopt more open communications styles to instigate more frequent dialogue and interactions with employees at all levels and provide opportunities for employees to contribute ideas and also given due recognition if these are implemented successfully.

Digital tools can also be used to increase the interaction between executives and employees, for example BP's SatNav for leadership app helps people identify and connect with other business leaders and subject specialists in the company to encourage networking which is an approach that can be employed by other large organisations. Increasing the visibility and interaction between executives and employees will invariably cause employees to become more self-directing and eventually result in driving improvements in productivity and creativity.

In this context, leadership is viewed as a collective responsibility rather than a solo activity, involving creating leadership forms, structures and mechanisms for sharing power and responsibility with people at all levels of the organisation. Transforming the leadership style across the organisation to a more collaborative, inclusive and transparent approach will enable employees to feel appreciated and recognised as contributors to the future growth of the company; it will also help to consolidate successes and open avenues for challenging unproductive tendencies which can hinder long-term growth. Accenture, for example, has evolved its leadership philosophy towards a stewardship mantra where everyone is considered to be a leader and given the responsibility to understand the value-drivers and make decisions to support the mission of the entire organisation.[8] This involved creating an environment of empowerment for employees to challenge ineffective processes and to offer creative alternatives; encouraging open dialogue at all levels of the organisation to help unearth any critical issues that can hinder effective customer service and providing the avenue for employee to understand all important processes and how to apply them effectively to drive value for the organisation.

Culture and values: The realigned structures and systems also need to be integrated with and supportive of the organisation's shared values and culture, such that middle managers and employees remain motivated and committed to receiving and sharing new ideas across the organisation to drive productivity and innovation. Any perceived lack of congruence between the structures and systems of the organisation and its culture, values and processes will generate low integrity in the system, and with low integrity, the organisation will enter a degenerative cycle. For instance, where core values for an organisation are based on teamwork and collaboration, but the reward system is out of sync and focuses on individuals rather than team levels, then the reward system will not support the operating values and will trigger low integrity, unfairness and lack of trust in the system. Any inconsistencies between an organisation's stated values and its behaviours is quickly picked up by employees who then react with low motivation and put in less discretionary effort towards achieving organisational goals. Reward systems must also build in some degree of flexibility for experimentation, risk-taking and creativity and even for early identification of failure. Reward systems at 3M build some degree of tolerance for mistakes and encourage learning by holding forums for employees to discuss barriers encountered on unsuccessful projects.[9]

A good example of alignment of values with reward system is Microsoft's HoloLens project which was carved out as a high-risk project initiated by employees with an appetite for risk. Due to the successful outcome of the project, the team members involved have been rewarded through rapid promotion to senior positions to drive creativity and innovation in other areas of the business.[10]

Shifting entrenched habits, structures and systems and the underlying assumptions is always a herculean task, but these must be addressed to remove the behavioural bottlenecks that can hinder the commitment and productivity levels necessary for delivering strategic initiatives successfully. Executives must therefore support and work closely with direct reports by conduct reviews to determine where the undesirable structures and systems and values are still entrenched to ensure that adequate measures are implemented across the organisation to embed the desirable approach required to deliver any value-centric initiatives. This may require the top executive team members to revisit their operating values, and reaffirm their shared vision and make the personal adjustments necessary to ensure that their behaviours are congruent with organisational values in their everyday interactions with employees and in their decision-making.

Intel's successful shift in strategy from a hardware company to a connected device, cloud and data centre company is underpinned by the GROW (Growing Relationships, Opportunities, and Wins) initiative which is a neuroscience-based approach based on actionable habits aimed at creating new behaviours to enable the organisation to evolve its organisation's culture and values, and to create an environment where employees can develop a growth mind-set to drive innovation[11].

An approach adopted by Exxon Mobil to implement a cultural and behavioural transformation programme has been useful in shifting and embedding desired values (refer to figure 6.3). Executives and senior leaders combine compelling storytelling (which was discussed in detail in Chapter 3) and experiential learning to embed desired behaviour and cultural change. Executives play an active role in the entire process, which involves experiencing an event in the workplace (processes, behaviours, or conversations), interpreting the results, identifying behaviours that need changing, sharing this with peers and direct reports (using storytelling techniques to highlight any incongruous or desirable behaviours and their impact on others), evaluating the impact of these on organisational outcomes and making further changes in behaviour until the target level of transformation is achieved.

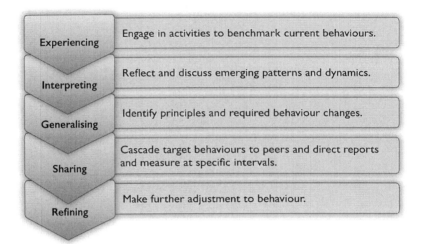

Experiencing — Engage in activities to benchmark current behaviours.

Interpreting — Reflect and discuss emerging patterns and dynamics.

Generalising — Identify principles and required behaviour changes.

Sharing — Cascade target behaviours to peers and direct reports and measure at specific intervals.

Refining — Make further adjustment to behaviour.

Figure 6.3 **Key steps in Exxon Mobil's cultural and behavioural transformation programme.**

Adopting this approach to driving cultural transformation anchors the expectations of executives, senior leaders and employees and sets a benchmark of mutually acceptable behaviour against which executives, leaders and employees are to be evaluated.

Embedding a collaborative leadership structure and culture can also facilitate effective decision-making at the strategic and tactical levels as important business decisions require the acquisition and integration of information (complete or incomplete) at the point of decision-making. Where the available information is incomplete, executives have to incorporate a large amount of assumptions which can lead to wrong decision-making with colossal consequences.

An organisational structure and culture that enables transfer of information from front-line staff to top management can enable executives to make important decisions based on fewer assumptions. The proximity of front-line employees to markets, customers, products and services and technology enables them to capture information which can be combined with other sources of data to improve the prediction/satisfaction of customer preferences, trends and needs.

This culture allows executives to access crucial information which can be combined with insight from data analytics and real-time information from front-line employees to make informed decisions about how to position the organisation to benefit from current and future opportunities. The criticality of acting swiftly on information to drive business value is supported by Whitney Hischier, Haas School assistant dean, Center for Executive Education UC Berkeley Center for Executive Education (CEE), who notes that 'many companies are steeped in a culture of deep analysis, with lots of data required to make decisions. To stay in the pace of the world today you have to understand how the outside world impacts your business and you have to go by gut. If you wait for all the data to be processed, your competitors will have already made the decision and moved on'.[12]

The atmosphere that permeates the organisations that embed a structure and culture that enables transfer of information is one of questioning and reflection and challenging of existing and predicted business models across all levels. This allows executives to have early indications of when business models are no longer relevant so that action can be taken to modify these models to provide better revenue generation and long-term value.

Organisations with a strong employee engagement climate can also use reverse psychology to speed up decision-making processes by getting staff to "think like" customers to help generate innovative products and services. For example, Adobe launched an internal initiative dubbed Experience-a-thon to allow employees to complete customer validation tests on Adobe products, not from their viewpoint as employees, but as users during its move from physical software to a cloud-based model which helped to improve the product development timescales and minimise the time to market the product.[13]

Knowledge exchange: Technology can be leveraged to drive knowledge exchange at all levels of the organisation to facilitate the successful execution of value-centric initiatives. IBM, Cisco and ABB, for instance, provide intranets, learning channels and other knowledge-sharing platforms at both the executive level and across the organisation to disseminate lessons learnt to stimulate and embed new ideas to drive organisational value and growth. Using data analytics, organisations can rationalise information on knowledge-share, incubate innovative ideas and highlight best practices which can be leveraged to drive value-centric initiatives. However, the greater levels of collaboration and connectedness that knowledge exchange platforms provide can also result in excessive employee burnout and therefore executives and leaders should draw on emotional intelligence capabilities to ensure that work design is well structured to promote employee well-being.

Operational level: Middle managers at the operational level need to demonstrate collaborative leadership behaviours to embed the enabling environment to the point that front-line employees are empowered and motivated to contribute towards the achievement of organisational goals. Adequate coaching must be provided by senior managers to middle managers so they can be more proactive in providing front-line employees with the required knowledge, information, resources, reasonable autonomy, recognition and reward to execute value-centric initiatives.

For example, at GlaxoSmithKline (GSK), a coaching centre of excellence has been created which initially involved executives and leaders at SVP, VP and other levels, allowing the organisation to standardise and subsequently make the practice accessible to employees at all levels to embed values and behaviours congruent with its strategic intentions.[14] The standardisation and roll out was achieved after all the executives were trained to offer coaching to their direct reports and once a critical mass of coaching experts was created, there was sufficient capacity within the organisation to offer coaching to all level of employees.

Boeing has also developed an internal coaching programme for emerging executives with the support of senior executives, which involves reflective and learning transfer reviews that are aimed at driving behaviour change and developing the capabilities required to unravel the challenges which can hinder productivity and effectiveness.[15] The effectiveness of this programme stems from the opportunity for coaches to co-coach with other more experienced counterparts, providing the opportunity for participants to apply their skills to real business challenges under the supervisions of others to galvanise their capabilities before embarking on solo assignments.

Middle managers must also be empowered and supported to engage in frequent leader-employee interactions (such as occasional meetup sessions with the team leaders in an informal setting over breakfast or lunch, interactive webinars, providing regular feedback on internal social media, and by organising 'Google Cafés', which are interactions sessions between leaders and cross-departmental teams to generate conversations on work issues as well as providing an avenue for recreation) specifically aimed at solidifying and enhancing employees' commitment and motivation levels. Pixar's success in the entertainment industry has been attributed to greater leader-member interactivity and diffusion of collaborative leadership at all levels where creative ideas are encouraged at all levels. All of these measures must be backed by a fair culture and a reward comprehensive system that considers both non-monetary and psychological elements and encompasses compensation, benefits, recognition and appreciation.

It is also important to instil a strong sense of accountability at the operational level by cascading objectives related to value-centric initiatives at the divisional, departmental and employee levels to provide visibility of contributions made towards achieving short- and long-term objectives. For example, at Twitter Inc., cross-functional collaboration through an effective combination of contextual leadership and deployment of smart technology enables a wider dissemination of project performance data status, success and failure to drive effective decision-making and swift action to drive productivity and innovation.[16]

Setting cross-departmental/divisional performance targets to trigger collaboration across various functions/divisions and departments can also be useful in cementing and embedding the right behaviours across the organisation. HR departments have a role to play in supporting executives and managers at all levels in the identification and validation of the correct performance management systems and measures that will feed into this process of increasing cross-functional collaboration.

Building a critical mass of middle managers capable of championing strategic interventions at the operational level will enhance employee motivation and commitment levels, as the source of motivation is not from a distance (i.e. the top executives) but from leaders who interact with employees on a daily basis and can directly influence the levels of discretionary effort at the operational level whereby employees explore avenues to drive continuous improvements and create innovative products and services. Greater leader-member interactions at the operational level will also create double-loop learning, resulting in adaptability, which enhances the enabling environment for employees to make further contributions towards organisational goals. Once this trend of extra-discretionary effort boosted by the enabling environment is embedded within the organisation, the organisation will be positioned for consistent delivery of customer-centric products and services which enhance market share, sales growth and profitability – and eventually translate into organic growth. However, owing to several factors such as attrition in staff, movements of staff across the organisation, general operational challenges and rapid growth pressures, there is a possibility for organisations to revert to non-collaborative states or silo mentality, stifling productivity, innovation and the responsiveness that characterises start-up and disruptive organisations. Cultivating a start-up mentality will help executives and other leaders to encourage a mind-set where technological perspectives are pursued in order to create more value-centred products, including regular customer validation to develop products and services that enhance customer experience. Start-ups engage in regular customer validation activities to ensure that the limited funds available to them are optimised to deliver products that will exceed customer expectations and give them a footing in existing markets. In the rapidly evolving digital landscape, businesses must constantly re-evaluate customer experience touch points and deliver more personalised experiences in order to stand out from the competition. Executives must also continually review the state of collaboration effectiveness across departments and divisions that have strategic impact on the growth trajectory of the organisation and ensure any blockers to the proper alignment of the structure, culture and value drivers are removed. This process should be extended to include assessment of engagement levels and collaboration between critical functions within the organisation and any external strategic ecosystem partners. Collaboration and engagement levels are higher in organisations with a start-up mentality because they cultivate the same sense of urgency, excitement and survival that start-ups need to drive innovation and power themselves to growth. For instance, Siemens is establishing a start-up mentality through an initiative named Next47 by building stronger ecosystem collaborating with competitors, academic institutions and research organisations, and by stimulating internal leadership creativity through the Siemens Technology and Innovation Council which consists of internationally experienced and respected experts from the research and scientific communities responsible for analysing and monitoring strategic topics in the areas of technology and innovation that will have an impact on Siemens' business.[17]

The Next47 initiative, which revolves around five interconnected themes (AI, Blockchains, distributed electrification, autonomous machines, and connected e-mobility), will encourage upwards transmission of ideas from all levels of the organisation, moving away from the silo mentality that is often endemic in large global conglomerates.[18]

Organisations that consistently realign their structure and culture to correspond with value-drivers are more likely to be well-positioned to benefit from long-term growth and to recover faster from economic shocks. This is exemplified by Statoil (previously known as Equinor), the Norwegian international energy company with operations in 36 countries. In 2010, Equinor began a transformation journey when it realised that traditional leadership and management practices were no longer relevant in today's competitive climate where organisations are operating in business environments characterised by more complexity, uncertainty and unpredictability. It implemented innovative alternatives to traditional management, which included abolishing traditional budgets and calendar-based management in favour of more decentralized and agile processes.

Although Equinor had always considered itself as a values-based and people-oriented organisation, over the years of growth, the consolidation of traditional management processes led to increased bureaucracy and rigidity to the extent that the gap between leadership principles and management processes widened and started to impact on organisational performance. Equinor responded by implementing a significant change initiative to drive simplification and renewal, to ensure that organisational and individual capability was at the core of the business.

In addition to the new change initiative, Equinor's leadership and management systems were distilled into a document known as the 'Equinor Book' – articulating all the principles, requirements and recommendations which support the organisation in fulfilling the tasks required to achieve its strategic objectives. The Equinor Book sets the foundation for how the organisation develops its executive and wider leadership capabilities, conducts business and sets standards for the organisational culture, behaviours, delivery of strategic initiatives and business model. It also provides clarity about what is required and expected of leaders across the organisation and sets the framework for developing the leadership capabilities at all levels to achieve the intended strategic objectives.[19]

At the launch of the new organisational structure and systems, which was dubbed 'Ambition to Action', Helge Lund, Equinor's ex-CEO described it in the following terms: 'We have a management model which is very well-suited to dealing with turbulence and rapid change. It enables us to act and reprioritise quickly so that we can fend off threats or seize opportunities'.[20] The changed structure and systems, coupled with the clear articulation of leadership principles and executive development efforts, have yielded positive results with Equinor reporting 25 per cent reduction of operational and administrative expenses per barrel of oil produced in 2016.[21] This allows the organisation to be resilient in a low-cost oil price environment. Equinor continues to leverage its new organisational structure and systems by investing in executive and leadership development in order to deliver strong operational performance across all business areas, as well as implementing measures to generate high production efficiency. This has also positioned Equinor to generate and develop innovative solutions across the organisation. For example, the organisation is capitalising on this new structure by implementing innovative programmes such as the Cap-X subsea drilling technology and initiating new ideas such as the snake-like swimming robots. Cap-X aims at increasing the efficiency of and reducing the costs of subsea oil extraction by up to 30% compared to conventional installations which will enable Equinor to implement a 'plug and play' solution on sea beds and enable flexibility in terms of operating from vessels instead of rigs.[22] The snake-like swimming robots initiative, on the other hand, which was launched in partnership with external partners, is geared towards significantly cutting costs in subsea oil exploration and mining.[23] All of these initiatives have been successful partly owing to the strict enforcement of the leadership principles and development framework enshrined within the 'Equinor Book', which articulates the value creating principles and leadership principles which are broadly summarised into three simple business imperatives: shaping the future – by looking for opportunities to improve the operations and business, and acting on them; empowering people – by setting and communicating a clear direction, trusting people to deliver and engaging across boundaries and; Delivering results – by making a difference and adding value by demonstrating safety leadership and commercial instinct.

Blackberry's path to recovery following its decline in the mobile handset sector has been predicated by refocusing on its core business drivers and transitioning into a new organisational and operating structure which enables greater focus on services, mobility solutions and software, established on a more efficient business model to support new transformational and growth objectives.[24] The restructuring has been underpinned by setting a new organisational culture but as CEO, John Chen, describes 'changing one's behaviour is like changing muscle memory – It takes time".[25] The culture change is also underpinned by setting congruent values with managers empowered through the organisation's 'Global Reward and Recognition Program' which rewards employees for exceptional performance and innovative contribution to organisational performance.[26] The reward system which encompasses a combination of financial and non-financial rewards as well as, recognition has been instrumental in bringing about the desired culture change, given that an organisations total reward system drives cultural transformation directly by selectively reinforcing certain beliefs, norms and values consistently demonstrated by employees.[27] In essence, executives can design rewards systems to align with expected values and norms to help propel and shift the culture to a desirable state. When a reward system is made integral of the cultural transformation process this should be consistently applied across all levels of the organisations including executives as any deviation or departure from the norm will send mix signals to employees about the validity of the dominant shared pattern of behaviour and hence reverse some of the gains in the cultural transformation (see figure 6.4).

In addition to the successful organisational/operational restructuring efforts, Blackberry has propelled itself out of the decline in the mobile market through effective integration of strategic acquisitions of organisations such as Good Technology, WathcDox and AtHoc to deepen user experience across hardware and software technology, including security and applications. The organisation has also departed from its previous strategy of going solo on some of its propositions (which was the approach adopted by Blackberry when it was running the propriety software of the mobile phone business) and has embraced the ecosystem model by forging partnerships with Qualcomm, Delphi Automotive and Ford Motor to develop innovative new systems.[28]

Blackberry has maintained the path to recovery by refocusing its core business drivers and moving into a new organisational and operating structure which not only allows executives to develop a compelling business model but also enables them to create an enabling environment where employees can be motivated to effectively implement strategic initiatives to drive value and long-term growth instead of falling into complete oblivion like Nokia and Kodak, which became victims of the VUCA environment and disruptive technology (as discussed in Chapter 1).

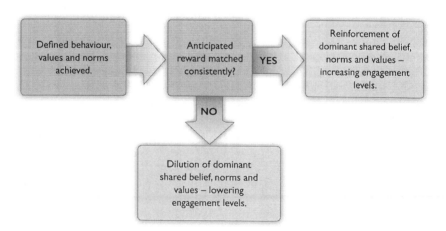

Figure 6.4 Value systems, rewards and culture impact relationships.

In summary, this chapter has outlined the important steps that executives need to implement at the strategic, operational and tactical levels to align the organisational architecture in order to enhance the successful delivery of strategic initiatives arising from executive development programmes by orchestrating and embedding an enabling environment for the front-line staff who are responsible for delivering strategic initiatives necessary for creating value and growth to be well positioned to functioning effectively.

Summary of key points

Investment in executive development will fail to yield maximum benefit unless efforts are taken to align the organisational architecture to allow effective transfer of dynamic capability from executives through the leadership chain to the frontline where the execution of strategic necessary for creating value and growth occurs.

This requirement for the realignment of organisational architecture will become more pronounced as organisations move into the digital economy where business models will be under regular scrutiny owing to intense competitiveness across maturing and emerging markets.

Executives will need to hone some core capabilities before embarking on the realignment of organisational architecture and some of the most effective executive development modalities that can be beneficial at this stage include; simulations (on managing complex changes and scenarios), ethical and unconsciousness bias training, deep-dive reviews, reflection learning exercises (prediction of possible challenging questions and scenarios and response plans), and coaching on goal achievement and effective change management.

Executives need decisiveness efficacy to evaluate the most effective architecture that will deliver the current and projected future organisational growth profile which must be combined with change leadership to champion and create the critical mass of key employees within the organisation to galvanise support for the change required to drive efficient delivery of the preferred option.

Successful delivery of the suitable architecture will also be dependent on executives' ability to break strategy intents into tangible steps that can be implemented across business units/divisions, focusing on results, instilling cross-functional working, without sacrificing the levels of inclusiveness, ethical conduct and integrity necessary for bonding people together during challenging transition from the old to the new paradigm.

Realigning the organisational architecture to facilitate effective execution of strategic initiatives must feature prominently on the board agendas so that entrenched political positions and blockers to the successful implementation can be resolved at the highest level of the organisational hierarchy.

Executives need to invest time in developing greater engagement with and preparing direct reports (top-level managers two to three tiers below) as another crucial step to ensure successful implementation of strategic initiatives carved out of executive development programmes.

A significant part of the action plans formulated at the strategic level will be implemented at the tactical level to address the gaps between value-centric initiatives and the existing organisational architecture (structure, systems, culture and values).

This will require refinement of key elements of the organisational architecture such as the structure, system, culture and value systems to engage senior and middle managers at the forefront of creating the enabling environment required for successful execution of value-centric initiatives across the organisation.

At the operational level, middle managers need to demonstrate collaborative leadership behaviours to embed the enabling environment to the point that front-line employees are empowered and motivated to contribute towards the achievement of organisational goals.

Coaching can be targeted by senior managers to enable middle managers to be more proactive at providing front-line employees with the required knowledge, information, resources, reasonable autonomy, recognition and reward to execute value-centric initiatives.

Middle managers must also be empowered and supported to engage in frequent leader-employee interactions specifically aimed at solidifying and enhancing employees 'commitment and motivation levels. All of these must be backed by a fair culture and a reward system.

Organisations must consistently realign their structure and culture to value-drivers to enable them to be well positioned to benefit from long-term growth and to recover faster from economic shocks and disruptive competitors.

References

1. Raphael Savalle, 'ROA matters: why P&G, Nestle and Danone are in trouble' (*Cnsumer Goods Technology* 22 June 2016) https://consumergoods.com/roa-matters-why-pg-nestle-and-danone-are-trouble-0 (last accessed 30 July 2017).
2. Seeking Alpha, 'Procter & Gamble: Being Outclassed By A $2.4 Billion Tiny Belgian Company' (Seeking Alpha Security Analysis 10 November 2015) https://seekingalpha.com/article/3672376-procter-and-gamble-outclassed-2_4-billion-tiny-belgian-company (last accessed 30 July 2017).
3. Bruce Rogers, 'Why 84% Of Companies Fail At Digital Transformation' (Forbes 7 January 2016) https://www.forbes.com/sites/brucerogers/2016/01/07/why-84-of-companies-fail-at-digital-transformation/#6137a552397b (last accessed 31 July 2017).
4. Roland Moore-Colyer, 'Microsoft's Digital Transformation Missive Is A Slow-Burn Evolutionary Strategy' (*Silicon UK* 2 November 2017) https://www.silicon.co.uk/cloud/microsoft-digital-transformation-224169?inf_by=5a4758e9671db8fe0a8b47b4 (last accessed 31 November 2017).

5. Alexander Schuhmacher, Markus Hinder and Oliver Gassmann, *Value Creation in the Pharmaceutical Industry: The Critical Path to Innovation* (Wiley 2016) 356.

6. Dina Bass and Ian King, 'Inside Microsoft's Plan to Bring AI to its Holo-Lens Goggles New HoloLens processor will let mixed reality goggles recognize speech and images' (Microsoft) https://developer.microsoft.com/en-us/windows/mixed-reality/academy (last accessed 31 November 2017).

7. Daimler, Change the game Leadership 2020, (Daimler Careers) https://www.daimler.com/career/thats-us/leadership2020/ (last accessed 31 November 2017).

8. Keith Johnston, 'Three Powerful Leadership Lessons from Accenture' (True North Leadership 30 June 2017) http://www.truleadership.com/three-powerful-leadership-lessons-from-accenture/ (last accessed 31 January 2018).

9. Lisa Bodell, 'Why You Didn't Meet Your Innovation Goals' (Strategy +Business 25 February 2015) https://www.strategy-business.com/blog/Why-You-Didnt-Meet-Your-Innovation-Goals-in-2014?gko=b7294 (last accessed 31 January 2018).

10. Carol Dweck and Kathleen Hogan, 'How Microsoft Uses a Growth Mindset to Develop Leaders' (*Harvard Business Review* 7 October 2016) https://hbr.org/2016/10/how-microsoft-uses-a-growth-mindset-to-develop-leaders (last accessed 31 November 2017).

11. Deb Bubb,'To survive and thrive we all must grow' (Intel, 8 February 2016) https://blogs.intel.com/jobs/2016/02/to-survive-and-thrive-we-all-must-grow/ (last accessed 30 December 2017).

12. UC Berkeley Center for Executive Education, 'Interdisciplinary Leadership Program Prepares Statoil Executives for Global Challenge' (Hass Berkeley Leading through Innovation 2016) https://haas.berkeley.edu/strategicplan/culture/lti/executive-education.html (last accessed 30 December 2017).

13. Kelvin Claveria, '4 digital transformation strategy examples, and what you can learn from them' (*Vision Critical* 10 February 2017) https://www.visioncritical.com/digital-transformation-strategy-examples/ (last accessed 30 December 2017).

14. Magdalena Mook, 'Creating a coaching culture from within' (*HR Magazine* 17 February 2017) http://hrmagazine.co.uk/article-details/creating-a-coaching-culture-from-within (last accessed 30 December 2017).

15. Howard Morgan, Phil Harkins and Marshall Goldsmith, *The Art and Practice of Leadership Coaching: 50 Top Executive Coaches Reveal their secrets* (Wiley 2011) 265.

16. Melissa Daimler, 'Why Leadership Development has to happen on the Job' (Harvard Business Review, 16 March 2016) https://hbr.org/2016/03/why-leadership-development-has-to-happen-on-the-job (last accessed 12 December 2017)

17. Siemens AG, 'Siemens to strengthen innovation and technology expertise' (Siemens AG Press Release, 3 December 2014) https://www.siemens.com/press/en/pressrelease/?press=/en/pressrelease/2014/corporate/pr2014120080coen.htm (last accessed 12 December 2017).

18. By Kathleen Maher, 'For Siemens, innovation starts in the USA: Digitize it, automate it, electrify it, communicate with it, analyze it' (*Graphic Speaks* 7 June 2017) http://gfxspeak.com/2017/06/07/siemens-innovation-start/ (last accessed 12 December 2017).

19. Statoil, 'The Statoil Book' (Statoil Ver 4.0 2017) https://www.statoil.com/content/dam/statoil/documents/the-statoil-book/StatoilBook_v4.0_ENG.pdf (last accessed 12 December 2017).

20. Bjarte Bogsnes, 'Taking reality seriously: towards a more self-regulating management model at Statoil' (Management Exchange 28 November 2011) https://www.managementexchange.com/story/taking-reality-seriously-towards-more-self-regulating-management-model-statoil (last accessed 12 December 2017).

21. Statoil, 'Annual Report and Form 20-F 2016' (Statoil 2017) https://www.statoil.com/content/dam/statoil/documents/annual-reports/2016/statoil-2016-annual report-20-F.pdf.pdf (last accessed 12 December 2017).

22. Statoil, 'Statoil launches new subsea concept' (Statoil News 26 June 2016) https://www.statoil.com/en/news/statoil-launches-new-subsea-concept.html (last accessed 12 December 2017).

23. Statoil, 'Collaboration on swimming robots for subsea maintenance' (Statoil News 28 June 2016) https://www.statoil.com/en/news/collaboration-swimming-robots-subsea-maintenance.html (last accessed 14 December 2017).

24. John Chen, 'Blackberry CEO outlines new strategy' (*The Globe and Mail* 25 March 2017) https://www.theglobeandmail.com/report-on-business/blackberry-ceo-the-journey-has-just-begun/article16125601/ (last accessed 16 December 2017).

25. Martin Bauman, 'BlackBerry CEO: Innovation key to company's turnaround' (*570 News* 17 September 2015) http://www.570news.com/2015/09/17/blackberry-ceo-innovation-key-to-companys-turnaround/ (last accessed 16 December 2017).

26. Nirmal K. Sethia and Mary Ann Von Glinow, 'Managing Organizational Culture by Managing the Reward System' (University of Southern California – Center for Effective Organisations 1994) https://ceo.usc.edu/files/2016/09/1984_16-g84_16-Managing_Organizational_Culture.pdf (last accessed 16 December 2017).

27. Blackberry, 'Corporate Responsibility Report 2015 & 2016' (Blackberry 2016) https://uk.blackberry.com/content/dam/bbCompany/Desktop/Global/PDF/corporate-responsibility/Corporate_Responsibility_Report_2015_2106.pdf (last accessed 16 December 2017).

28. Brian Deagon, 'BlackBerry Breaks Out on Strong Quarterly Earnings, Topping Estimates' (*Investors* 19 December 2017) https://www.investors.com/news/technology/blackberry-breaks-out-on-strong-quarterly-earnings-topping-estimates/ (last accessed 20 December 2017).

7

Measuring the impact of executive development on organisational performance

As discussed in Chapter 3, executive cohorts tend to have a greater preference for informal or experience-based learning which tend to be situated within the workplace (e.g. coaching, reverse-mentoring, business simulations, networking, stretch projects, job rotations) compared to the formal counterpart (instructed-lead classroom-based sessions, web-based sessions, e-learning courses, curated content on learning management systems (LMS), workshops, seminars and webinars). It is more challenging to assess the impact of such informal learning modalities on organisational performance as they are less structured and melded into the workplace environment and therefore the acquisition, application and transfer of capabilities can often occur concurrently which complicates the ability to capture and track the effects of such interventions on organisational performance.

Competing priorities, lack of access to data, not knowing how to start and cost implications are amongst some of the frequently challenges cited by organisations for not measuring the impact of learning on organisational outcomes[1].

The challenge of measuring informal learning interventions is compounded further by the time lag between when executives engage in development programmes and how long it takes for them to master and apply capabilities to drive and embed value-centric initiatives. These factors, particularly the informal nature of executive development, render existing evaluation models such as the Kirkpatrick's four-level and Philip's five-level models (summarised in table 7.1 below) inadequate for this level of employees as they are simplistic and fail to cater for the informal nature of executive development.

These two popular models have inherent weaknesses and require refinement to make them suitable for evaluating executive development programmes as outlined below:

* Retrospective measurement of business impact and expected value creation.
* Limited applicability to informal learning/workplace learning which tends to be the most relevant to the executive cohort.

Table 7.1 Comparison between the Kirkpatrick's four-level and Philip's five-level models

Kirkpatrick's four-level Model	Philip's five-level Model
Level 1: Reaction: evaluates participants reaction to the training in terms of the degree of engagement and relevant to their current work	**Level 1.** Reaction, Satisfaction, & Planned Action - evaluates participant reaction to and satisfaction with the training program and participant's plans for action
Level 2: Learning: Assesses how participants acquired the knowledge, skills, attitude, confidence and commitment following participation in the training intervention	**2. Learning** - Assesses the skills and knowledge acquired from the training.
Level 3: Behaviour: Checks how participants apply new knowledge and learning to influence workplace situations.	**Level 3.** Application and Implementation – Evaluates the level of change gained from the training such as the on-the-job application, behaviour change, and implementation of new ideas.
Level 4: Results; Considers the outcomes of the training intervention on business results	**4. Business Impact** – Measures the improvement in business objectives arising from the training (taking into account any exigencies).
	Level 5. Return on Investment (ROI) - Compares the financial value accrued to the business with the costs of implementing the training programme

- No in-depth consideration of behaviour (and learning) anchoring, championing, transferring (sharing), embedding (team, division and organisation–wide) to provide the needed bridge and connection for validating the return of Investment assessments.
- Return on Investment evaluation (ROI) is not holistic enough and fails to incorporate the effects of intangibles such as enhancements in inter-departmental collaboration, cultural transformation) that are derived from effective executive development programmes.
- To address some of the limitations of existing measurement models and to align them for effective evaluation of executive development programmes, an alternative framework is offered by combining elements of the Kirkpatrick and Philip models supplemented by new ideas suitable for addressing informal learning. The resulting executive development evaluation model encapsulates five stages, as depicted in figure 7.1.

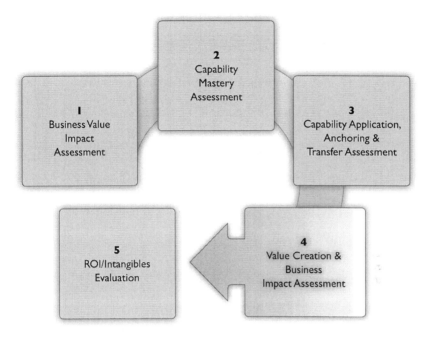

Figure 7.1 Executive development evaluation model.

Business value impact assessment: The first stage of evaluating executive development programmes must not dwell on reactive measures (focusing on post-intervention/training satisfaction evaluation and action planning for participants) as per the Kirkpatrick and Philip models (refer to Table 7.1 above) but focus more on predictive measures related to the anticipated business value impact of the development intervention. A split of 80:20 (predictive measures related to anticipated business value impact such as anticipated percentage of cost reduction at divisional/business level, target number of new innovations, number of new markets to be developed, decision-making speed and team transformation to operate in ecosystem environment (including any variants of the business value drivers discussed in Chapter 1) versus: reactive measures such as individual/team satisfaction scoring of the development intervention, suitability of the modality to closing identified capability gaps, suitability of the modality to level of executive cohort and overall effectiveness of the modality) is recommended to ensure that better focus is given to the value and growth factors during the evaluation process. This will ensure that the evaluation does not only provide a feedback loop for improving the executive development modalities but more importantly, check the connectedness of the development interventions to organisational value drivers, and set the expectations for return in investment evaluation.

Cisco's executive learning action programme provides a clear and upfront link between expected capabilities and value drivers and has established a cross-functional committee which oversees the link between executive development programmes and business impact. Some of the value drivers that have been considered in the past include acting within Cisco's executive expectations; driving innovation through cross-organisational collaboration; mastering industry and market competitive intelligence; developing strategic and operating plans; building diverse, high-performance business teams; and transforming the core business while innovating for the future.[2]

Cisco's approach exemplifies how other organisations can plan their executive development interventions effectively by capturing the value drivers proactively so that they can form part of the evaluation process. But too often some organisations make no provision for the identification and measurement of the predictive indicators which are crucial for assessing the business impact of development interventions and motivate executive participants to apply and transfer new capabilities into the work environment to drive improvements in business results.

At 3M, participants in executive and leadership development programmes have clear expectations of capabilities, which include value creation, profitability growth, acceleration of innovation, enhanced performance and leadership for execution.[3]

3M's Catalyst programme focuses on moving leadership development from a limited, time-based event to a continuous journey over 12 months to help embed the desired business capabilities and incorporates multiple face-to-face learning opportunities with senior executives, customers and other stakeholders which is augmented by blended learning with curated content from both online and mobile-enabled platforms. Participants also use real-time projects and spot coaching to develop their skills and the e-programs incorporate the company's award-winning 'Leaders developing others' approach which involves organisational leaders designing and delivering development programmes and expanded to include sessions led by taught-leaders in various fields, community leaders, customers and other stakeholders.[4]

Similarly, ExxonMobil's Advanced Leadership Program (ALP) helps transform proven leaders into global executives and has learning objectives which include: integration of processes and maximizing learning across borders, accelerating the transition from managing to leading in a global business, developing strategic perspective and vision, and developing the ability to communicate vision successfully in ways that enhance employee engagement and understanding—all of which are key global business drivers which impinge on the successful delivery of business models and value drivers.[5]

In partnership with Duke CE, Verizon has designed a blended learning programme based on experiential learning and customised simulation to drive the focus of senior and director-level executives towards long-term value creation.[6] The experiential component of the programme involves executives working within cross-business units and cross-functional teams to identify obstacles preventing the organisation from creating more shareholder value, and solutions are reported back to a panel of top executives.[7]

The programme provides executives with clear metrics for analysing how their decisions and actions affect shareholder value creation and each participant is required to submit an Individual Accountability Plan (IAP) - a detailed action plan which must be aligned with these 'value drivers'. The top two actions from the IAPs are selected, prioritised and monitored and reviewed on a regular basis until completion, with the support/supervisions of business unit presidents[8].

Evaluation of the predictive value drivers affected by the development programmes in the first phase of evaluation must be complemented by initial assessment of executives' capacity to transfer new insights, ideas and information across the business and the speed at which this can occur. This phase of evaluation also needs to consider any potential learning transfer implementation barriers and avenues for addressing them by the Chief Learning Officer or HR Director working with the executive team. By early consideration of the reactive and predictive indicators that need to be measured, executives and organisations can proactively plan how to capture the metrics from available organisational databases to link executive development programmes to value-centric initiatives. Consideration should also be given to any enabling factors such as reward systems, objective setting and performance review processes in this phase of evaluation. Other variables that should be evaluated at this stage include any goals/objectives that need to be changed/included to drive required behaviour changes at the individual executive, team and organisational levels.

Capability mastery: This phase of executive development evaluation focuses on measuring the extent to which the expected levels of capabilities, behaviours and attitudes have been mastered at the individual executive/team levels against baseline measures. The frequency, responsibilities and modes of assessment must be agreed beforehand (during the first evaluation stage) and responsibilities need to be cascaded to the CEO and board level to ensure effective coordination, evaluation, monitoring and implementation of actions to close capability gaps that are identified during the evaluation of capability mastery. Digital technology can be used to capture real-time feedback on executive performance. BP's SatNav for leadership app developed for business leaders enables users to receive anonymous feedback from their employees on their daily leadership performance.[9] One advantage of using the app is that it offers the capability to measure the impact of training on leaders, the team and the business which allows change in behaviour to match expected patterns from the team.

Accepting negative feedback can be difficult for some executives as often, some responses have personal connotations and can result in an emotive reaction instead of a rational interpretation. That said, executives need to embrace different reactions from each individual as long as the organisation is aware that there will always be a level of personality influence on the responses. This way, measures of behaviour change should be at an incremental level rather than at a specific target level, for example, a target can be set to achieve in excess of 60 per cent positive behaviour change (where applicable, adjustments can be made to reflect personality influences) in the first month, and then drive the target up to 70 per cent etc. and only reviewed on an exceptional basis.

Measurement process: data capture to assess the effectiveness of executive development initiatives should span the entire spectrum of the executive development evaluation model from capability mastery, right through to ROI. Suitability of data should be discussed and agreed with participants and other stakeholders and any combinations of organisational value drivers (business model optimisation, incremental and disruptive innovation, cost cutting and efficiencies, customer retention and acquisition, strategic partnerships and alliances, mergers and acquisitions) which will be impacted by the executive development intervention needs to be agreed upfront. The data can be captured from various organisational sources such as HR information systems (HRIS), customer satisfaction surveys, learning management system, performance management system, engagement surveys, productivity scorecards, innovation scorecards, safety performance scores, quality dashboards, and financial performance metrics.

AI-driven and learning analytics companies such as Zoomi, Kmi Learning, Echo360, Inc. and Gyrus Systems LLC are developing platforms for generating and analysing data based on learner's interactions during formal and informal settings which can help determine individual and group unique learning styles, preferences and any common patterns, including helping to determine possible approaches that will be unsuitable for certain executive cohorts and which are most effective. This approach can also allow data collected to be undertaken across different development interventions to determine how different cohorts and levels of executives respond to different interventions and also allow for development interventions to be redesigned addressing specific value-centred challenges faced by the organisation. The insights gained from the footprint of each learner or, indeed, groups of learners can be used to improve learning engagement levels through better personalisation of learning, and enhance learning transfer rates by ensuring that lessons learnt from previous learners are accounted for in designing new programmes. All of these will contribute towards an increased 'return on learning' for executives with similar levels of seniority or background and allow the organisation to become more proficient at modelling the possible business outcomes of different types of development interventions.

Application, anchor (embed) and transfer: This stage of evaluation is crucial for maximising the value from executive development programmes and must be given the highest focus. Data captured on capability mastery and changes in desired behaviours can prepare the grounds to assess application effectiveness and readiness for anchoring and transferring capabilities to influence value-centric initiatives. It will be beneficial for concrete evidence of capability application to be captured at the individual and team levels through learning journals and logs to help bridge the connection between acquisition and application from informal setting as these tend to occur concurrently. For example, executives can participate in a Hackathon with start-up entrepreneurs and acquire decision-making and strategic insight related to the sector which is then applied in the successfully acquisition of a disruptive innovator that generates quantifiable long-term benefits to an organisation. A well-documented learning journal will provide the link between these events, which can be used to justify further investments in this type of executive development intervention. The evaluation of application needs to consider the effectiveness of the channels and opportunities (e.g. leading/involvement in challenging assignments, special and innovative projects, (with cross-departmental collaborations), participating in strategic decision-making outside normal span of operation, leading negotiations in more complex environments (involving politicians, suppliers, and strategic partners), launching new businesses or developing emerging markets, leading new ventures with eco-system partners, leading a special task force to remove operational bottlenecks, and leading/participating in investor relations sessions), available within the organisations to apply newly acquired capabilities, behaviours/learning within the same or different division and any barriers encountered. Review of objectives at multiple levels to support the effective application and transfer of learning across the organisation and should be evaluated at this stage. Effective journaling, capturing or recording of the learning journey, including reflections, challenges encountered and how they were resolved enables the review process to occur effectively and should be accounted for during the design stage of the development intervention, including consideration of the format this information will be stored and retrieved without causing any data protection and privacy issues. Details of the capability application, anchoring and transfer can be implemented via technological platforms such as learning management systems (LMS) and will be subject to similar considerations as the journaling process. One key benefit of using technology platforms is that it helps drive value creation across the wider business through sharing both best practice and pain points.

At 3M, the anchoring and transfer of learning is facilitated through multiple platforms and this process transcends the executive level to embrace an organisation-wide approach.

This includes the provision of various platforms and channels such as intranet knowledge platforms, databases, formal learning networks, best practice descriptions/processes and avenues for idea management.

- *Intranet knowledge platforms databases*: Executives and employees are provided access to a 'WorkCenter', which is a collection of tools, systems and processes used routinely in daily work practices to successfully complete projects/work assignments in an employee's functional work area, thereby providing the means of learning capture.
- *Formal learning networks*: The Global Learning Network (GLN) is 3M's corporate learning management system; it is a one-stop electronic learning centre that helps executives, including employees, to enrol in, deliver, track and report on learning activities. GLN serves the learning needs of 3M business units, plants and learning organisations globally. The tracking and reporting functionality of the GLN enables executives to capture and share the impact of their learning with peers and employees to drive enhanced business value and growth.

- *Best practice descriptions/processes*: 3M cascades best practices via its Tech Forum and Engineering Technology Organization (ETO). These and other platforms provide an extensive network of expertise through specialised chapters focused on 3M's core technologies and emerging markets. This allows executives and employees in research and development, manufacturing and other parts of the supply chain to collaborate and drive innovation globally across the organisation.

Idea management at 3M is driven differently across the company depending on organisational needs and what works best for a specific business unit/division, taking a balanced approach between current and anticipated customer needs. Examples of successful platforms which has been implemented by 3M include, Spark, Innovation Live, Wiki Enterprise and other 3M internal and external social media channels. All of these systems are implemented and available globally to share best practices and to support organisational communications, learning and knowledge management. These also enable executives to drive information and knowledge to the right people across the organisation to stimulate value creation and growth and continue to evaluate the pros and cons of these platforms and decide which one to invest in depending on how these align to current and future needs.

The degree to which the collective outcomes from executive development programmes (new ideas, behaviours and capabilities) are anchored at a divisional/department level needs to be measured. Anchoring which involves validation and consolidation of new capabilities allows executives the space to reflect on and refine processes before eventual roll-out. This must be followed by the speedy and successful transfer/diffusion of these outcomes to stimulate value-centric initiatives across the organisation. This step of the evaluation should focus on establishing the extent to which learning and behaviours have been disseminated across the organisation or transferred to other regions/divisions to drive value.

At Cisco, executives share learning experiences via the Cisco Leadership Channel, an interactive web-based programme that features leadership-oriented content. The channel serves as an online library, chat room and social network for members of the executive action learning forum. It also has tracking functionalities that provides valuable data on how many people access the channel, what areas they visit, how long they stay and how often they return. The Cisco leadership channel:

- Provides common messaging to the director and executive populations on emerging industry trends, developments on critical innovation projects and updated on other internal issues.
- Serves as a virtual 'common room' allowing discussion about common topics via forums, including feedback on guess speakers at executive forums, etc.

- Collects and consolidates all chatroom discussions and organises them into an online resource with metrics for determining content relevance for different users.
- Uses web, video streaming and social networking technology to encourage a blended learning model/approach.

Anchoring should also take account of cultural sensitivities and geographic differences. One way to limit the effects of cultural sensitivities is to pilot these learning transfer initiatives within a division in a different geographic culture before final transfer is implemented across the organisation. The final steps in the evaluation process should focus on measuring the extent to which learning and behaviours have been embedded as 'business as usual' to drive the value creation process, and the extent to which refinements are made and fed back to adjust the executive development design and implementation process.

The data gathering and evaluation for the anchoring, transferring and embedding phase are likely to encompass a wider range of stakeholders (cross-functional) and the locus of evidence will shift to observing changes in the wider organisation beyond the scope of those executives immediately involved in the development programmes. This requires executives to engage and involve cross-functional and operational managers in the collection, analysis and dissemination of evaluation data and to structure the effort in a manner that targets the effects of executive development outcomes on value-centric initiatives. It is therefore important to ensure strong collaboration and communication across functions; as failure on these two fronts will hinder the pace and success of the expected benefits from executive development interventions.

Incremental business impact (short- and medium-term)

A useful means of counteracting the effects of the time lag between executive development programmes and the impact of learning on business transformation / outcomes is to break down the measures into intermediary (leading) indicators, short-term indicators and medium-term indicators.

Intermediate indicators: Intermediate or leading indicators focus on a range of parameters, including improvement in levels of collaboration and supportive leadership, degree of alignment of processes and systems (e.g. rewards) to learning transfer and application, employee engagement levels, leader – leader exchange (engagement) levels, leader – member exchange levels, executive, leadership and staff retention levels and diversity and inclusiveness levels. These indicators can be viewed as proxy measures or mediatory indicators which signal the effectiveness of executive development interventions/activities that affect short-term business measures.

Short-term business impact (6–12 months): Assessment of the short-term business impact of executive development programmes should focus on levels of

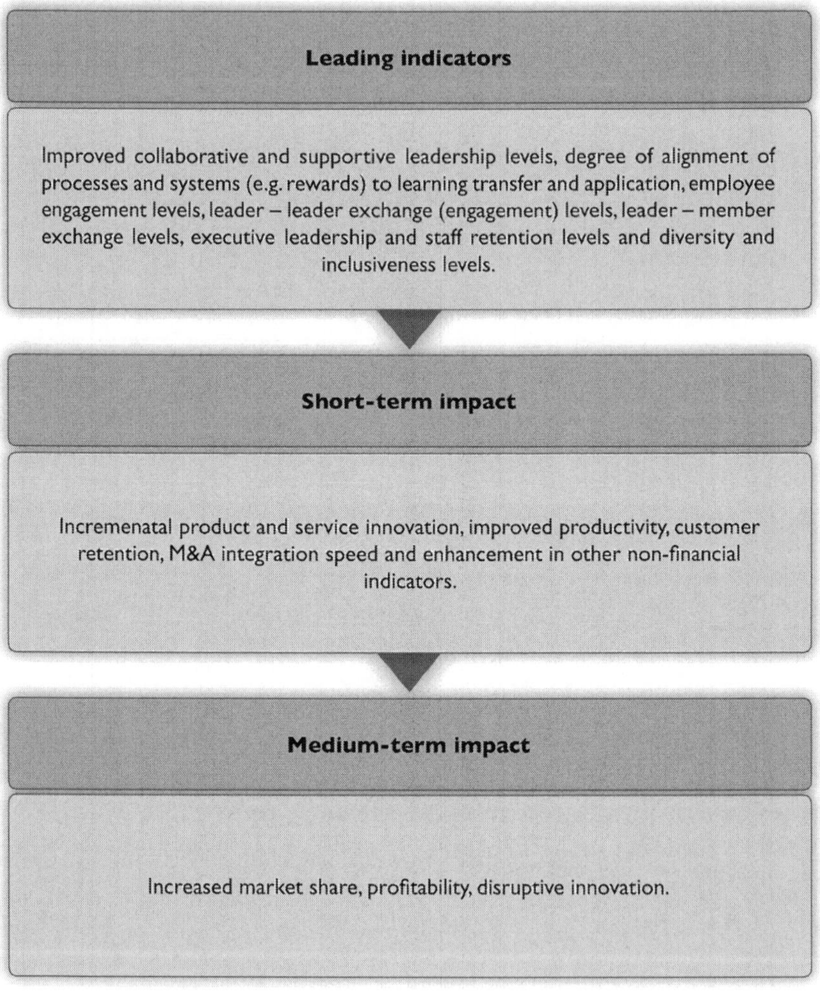

Figure 7.2 Incremental impact of executive development on organisational performance in the short, medium and long term.

improvement in product and service innovation, customer retention levels, M&A integration speed and other non-financial indicators that provide further visibility of the long-term value that is likely to accrue to the organisation.

Medium-term business impact (12–24 months): Enhancement of profitability and market share takes time to materialise following the application and transfer of executive development outcomes. It may take several months for an organisation to reap the full benefits and a 1–2-year timeframe is therefore not unusual. In measuring the medium-term business effects of executive development programmes, it is important to isolate any measurable effects of exogenous factors, such as seasonal sales and other cyclical factors.

ROI/ROE: Can we tell the full story of how the business impact/ROI was achieved? Provided all the evaluation stages of application, capturing, anchoring, transferring and embedding are followed, the assessment of the ROI and return on equity (ROE) of executive development programmes can be conducted with confidence. To enable effective ROI evaluation of executive development programmes and to allow effective replication in other environments and contexts, it is necessary to combine both quantitative (cost benefits on investment) and qualitative information (story behind the success).

Executive development programmes can be an expensive investment. For example, Cisco's budget for leadership development is approximately US$10 million per annum,[10] and it is important to evaluate the benefits (in terms of the business outcomes that result from these projects) to justify continuous investment. There always has to be the comparison to 'what if we had not invested?'. Would the business go backwards and into a decline? This is always a subjective topic but a continual challenge that executives have to face.

Building a robust estimate of executive development costs to enhance the accuracy of the ROI calculations necessitates the inclusion of indirect factors such as time taken away from everyday work by executives to engage in e-learning, travelling costs for informal networking events, cost of operating learning management systems, cost of job rotation programmes, cost allowance for delegating to less experienced staff whilst engaging in development programmes, cost of time taken off to engage in corporate university programmes, and cost associate with engaging external coaching / mentoring expertise. Cisco's executive action learning forum has rolled out several business concepts and transformation initiatives. One such initiative is the widely publicised SmartGrid, in which the company produced communications devices for the electricity delivery system. Cisco generated more than US$20 billion over a five-year period from this project.[11] Although each executive action learning forum costs between US$200,000 and US$300,000, the success of the leaders who attend the programme is measured through their return on investment to the business and in terms of their capacity to execute large-scale projects.[12] A global emerging technologies business in Bangalore, India, is another venture launched through the executive action learning forum and has generated revenues in excess of US$1 billion in the first three years. These examples demonstrate good returns on Cisco's investment in executive development programmes.

Comparing the executive development evaluation model to Kirkpatrick's (new world) evaluation and Philip's evaluation models

The various stages of the executive development evaluation model are juxtaposed against Kirkpatrick's four-level and Philip's five-level models to highlight how it can be applied to drive organisational value and growth (see table 7.2).

Table 7.2 The executive development evaluation model juxtaposed against Kirkpatrick's four-level and Philip's five-level models.

Kirkpatrick's (New World) Evaluation	Philip's Evaluation	Executive Development Evaluation
Reaction: Engagement, Relevance & Satisfaction	Reaction: Satisfaction and planned action.	**Value Impact Assessment (Predictive):** • **Value drivers affected** – Identifying the expected value drivers to be affected by this development assignment/ activity. • **Transferability** – Establishing the possibility for learning/ideas transfer across the business. • **Speed of implementation** –Ascertaining how quickly learning/ideas can be implemented to drive value. • **Barriers to implementation** – Identifying possible obstacles that will be encountered in implementing the ideas/learning across the business. • **Supporting mechanisms** – Identifying the processes and systems (e.g. rewards) required for successful application and transfer of learning/ideas. • **Business objectives affected:** Confirming the business objectives that need to be changed/included to drive the required capabilities and behaviours at individual executive and team levels (including direct reports).
Learning: knowledge, skills, attitude, confidence and commitment **Behaviour:** application on the job supported by required drivers such as processes and systems (e.g. rewards)	Learning: what skills, knowledge or attitudes have been changed and by how much. Job application and implementation: was there behaviour change and how did participant apply the learning to the job?	**Capability Mastery:** • **Capability mastery** – Assessing the degree to which consistent levels of value-transforming capabilities, behaviours and attitudes have been achieved at the individual executive/team levels. **Capability application and transferability:** • **Apply:** Identifying and confirming the opportunities for applying capabilities, behaviours/learning within a different context/division or project to drive value and monitoring of objectives at multiple levels. • **Capture** – Identifying the degree to which new learning/ideas have emerged and rationalise, capture and store within organisational systems.

Results: target outcomes and leading indicators (short-term observations and measurements)	Business impact; did on-the-job application produce measurable results?	• **Anchor:** Establishing the degree to which new learning/ideas are anchored at a divisional/department level to drive value and determine readiness for wider transfer. • **Transfer:** Establishing degree to which learning/ideas are disseminated across the organisation or transferred to other regions/divisions to drive value (making provision for localisation). • **Embed and refine:** Measuring the degree to which learning/ideas are embedded as business as usual to drive value. Identifying the frequency with which refinements are implemented and feedback into the executive development cycle. **Value Creation & Business Impact Assessment** **Leading indicators** • Productivity and innovation improvement levels. • Collaborative and supportive leadership culture. • Alignment of processes and systems (e.g. rewards) to learning transfer and application. • Employee engagement levels. • Leader – leader exchange (engagement) levels. • Leader – member exchange levels. • Readiness of leadership pipeline to assume future leadership roles. • Executive, leadership and staff retention levels. • Diversity and inclusiveness levels. **Business impact (6–12 months)** Innovation, customer retention, M&A integration.
N/A	ROI; did the monetary value of the results exceed the cost of the programme?	**Business impact (12–24 months)** Profitability and market share. **Return on Investment / Intangibles** - Complete story of how the business impact / ROI was achieved, including the intangible benefits gained in addition to the financial benefits generated.

The executive development evaluation model offers a more pragmatic framework than existing evaluation models at it targets both executive-level factors and wider organisational indicators.

It is important to ensure the right measures are developed, and these may vary across sectors and may be empirically developed based upon the emerging factors over a period of time – the Board and the Executives need to be patient with this and not 'cut it off at its knees' when they do not see the progress they expected, but be brave enough to stay the course – this can often be a challenge as other business drivers emerge during the implementation of different series of executive development programmes.

The executive development evaluation approach also provides a means of connecting executive development to clearly defined business drivers which can be translated into objectives and achievable goals and cascaded to multiple levels of an organisation. The focus of application and impact - to provide the proper focus throughout the organisation to drive business value - is also crystallised by this approach. This ensures that expectations are created for executive cohorts to clearly visualise why the executive development initiative is being undertaken and their role in the application, anchoring, transferring and embedding stages (learning touchpoints) to enhance the successful execution of value-centric initiatives. This allows data collection and capture (log-books, iPads), planning and any technology requirements to be built in much earlier, ensuring a flawless and efficient assignment of responsibilities to implement a robust measurement regime.

Business impact measurement

Given the centrality of the measurement process to the executive development investment, it is important that organisations devote the necessary resources and establish clear guidance on how this will be undertaken. This should take into consideration a number of factors which includes the data capturing process, evaluation options, segmentation and analysis of the data, normalisation and using the data for leveraging and closing gaps in the executive development process (summarised in figure 7.3) and are expanded upon below.

Data Capture: As already discussed in Chapter 3, the required evaluation data should be considered during the design phase of the executive development intervention and likely to be more difficult to capture if left towards the end of the evaluation. Due consideration should be given to how existing data can be presented in a comparable manner if the evaluation will involve executives in different geographical regions, and various performance thresholds and bandwidths should be agreed upfront with participation of executives during the design phase of the executive development initiative to avoid any ambiguities of expected performance. Significant effort may be required in agreeing how behavioural measures will be captured, anchored, transferred and embedded as this is one of the most important intangible benefits

Data Capture	Data capture data needs to take into acoount existing data sources and any additional information required and involve key stakeholders (CEO, C-suite and learning participants).
Evaluation options	Different variants of evaluation options; Standalone, Standalone (with isolation of exogenous factors), Peer to peer (normalised/ unnormalized), Peers (participating versus non-participating), and Different levels of executives (same intervention).
Segmentation & Analysis	Segmentation and analysis - business or geographic level to unearth similarities and difference, causation and correlations.
Normalisation	Normalisation needs to take into account exogenous factors such as Economic cycles, changes in market conditions, regulations and disruptive innovation.
Leverage & Close Gaps	Leverage Capabilities / Close gaps – leverage mastered capabilities to disrupt or close gaps to assure consistent growth.

Figure 7.3 Business Impact Evaluation Process.

of executive development interventions which is required to drive cultural transformation and disruptive business models.

Evaluation options: Evaluation of the business and ROI effects of executive development can be implemented with a number of variations. It can be standalone (without isolating the effects of exogenous effects). In this instance the evaluation will be based solely on the assessment of the crude return of investment figures without consideration of the effects of any noise or external factors which could skew the results. This is a low-cost solution and can be implemented very quickly without recourse to data analytics techniques or other complicated statistical analysis. Another approach is to employ the standalone evaluation of the return on investment computation with all the identifiable exogenous effects normalised. This approach will provide more accuracy but involves cross-departmental data collection and validation to identify all the possible range of exogenous factors that need to be stripped out of the computation to provide a normalised ROI position. The third approach involves comparing the performance differences (normalised or non-normalized) between participating peers (same or different cohorts). The fourth approach involves comparing the performance differences between participating peers and non-participating peers (with similar characteristics such as demographics, levels of seniority and business challenges), The fifth approach will be to compare the performance effects across different levels of executives (C-suite, direct reports and 3 levels below) based on participation in the same cluster of development interventions. All the five evaluation approaches (summarised in figure 7.4) can be segmented at the operational, geographical or business

Standalone (without isolating the effects of exogenous factors)	Standalone (with isolation of exogenous factors)	Peer to peer (normalised/ unnormalised)	Peers (participating versus non-participating)	Different levels of executives (same intervention)
• Relatively easier to implement than other approaches. • Cost effective as it does not involve excessive data collection and analysis. • Can offer quick results to inform rapid decision making. • No specialist statistical analysis required. • Results conflated by exogenous factors. • Suitable for quick evaluations to help redesign existing modalities or pilot new interventions.	• More expensive approach as it involves cross departmental input and support from a statistician. • More accurate results but more time consuming. • Suitable for long term evaluation/ panel data. • May be too complex to inplement by smaller organisations.	• Enables benchmarking to identify application effectiveness across peers. • Allows individual learning styles and preferences to be mapped. • Helps to locate any unique enablers & obstacles within departments, divisions and geographic regions.	• Allows comparison of inter/intra performance across divisions, departments and geographic regions. • Requires creating barriers to prevent leakage of information between participating and non-participating cohorts which may be difficult to implement. • The time lag required between different cohorts to allow for learning application and performance impact can delay building the critical mass in capabilities required to respond to any emerging threats.	• Suitable for particular interventions which can be deployed across all levels of the organisation. • Helps to identify modalities which are more suitable / unsuitable for certain levels of executives. • Common informal modalities may be more difficult to cascade to senior executives. • Cost benefit of the evaluation process may be low and may not add any additional benefit for organisations with a matured learning culture.

Figure 7.4 Evaluation options for executive development effects on organisational performance.

unit level depending on the size of the organisation. This will provide useful insight such as the effectiveness of different executive development modalities and how these can be tailored to meet the needs of specific cohorts, divisions or geographic regions to drive better return on investment.

Segmentation and analysis: Segmenting the evaluation at the business or geographic level will not only unearth the differential financial performance effects of the executive learning initiatives but will also help identify any cultural differences between operating units, lack of shared operating practices, limited cross-functional succession planning and any disparities in instilling a shared vision and operating practices across the company which will require further development interventions. This approach will also highlight any cluster of capabilities which have been mastered within certain divisions which can be leveraged to trigger disruptive business model innovation to drive long-term strategic growth. If conducted effectively, segmentation will allow organisations to gain insight into how to customise learning to address cultural sensitivities, behavioural biases and any ingrained silo mentality which can impede the implementation of cross-functional initiatives required to drive product and services in order to enhance organisational growth. The peer review (with participating cohorts) evaluation approach can also help identify any deficiencies in the range of development interventions offered to executives and serve as a feedback loop to influence the design, fine tuning and selection of appropriate development interventions to drive organisational value and growth.

Normalisation: The business impact and ROI data can be normalised to take into account any exogenous factors such as economic cycles, changes in market conditions, geographic factors, regulations and disruptive innovations which can either dilute or over-amplify the effects of the executive development interventions on performance. However, it is important to consider the additional cost implications for conducting complex normalisation analysis on the performance data and it may be beneficial to focus on relatively simpler approaches such as standalone evaluations without any normalisation of exogenous effects, or peer review with participating cohorts and peer review with non-participating cohorts as these approaches can still offer credible differential effects of executive development on business performance. The peer review with non-participating cohorts may be difficult to control owing to potential leakage/knowledge transfer of information about the development intervention (s) from the participating cohorts to their non-participating peers. The knowledge sharing that can occur between different cohorts can be a useful source of tacit knowledge which can help reshape the redesign of the development intervention but can be counterproductive if separation is required for the analysis. In order to create some of form of separation between the two cohorts (participating/non – participating) it may be necessary to stagger or phase the delivery of the development interventions by say a six monthly/annual (to allow sufficient time for behaviour change and application etc to occur) and this may be counterintuitive for many organisations expecting their executive teams to grasp capabilities in a speedy manner in order to proactively manage emerging threat from competitors cannot apply this approach. In any case, if an organisation opts to analyse the effects of executive learning on participating and non-participating cohorts in different geographical regions or departments, the impact of any favourable/unfavourable regulatory changes, increase in performance or revenue due to competitors going out of business and any events which cannot be directly attributable to enhanced capabilities of participating executive development should be stripped out of any data used for the comparison as part of the normalisation process.

In practice, establishing which specific factors to normalize including the estimation of associated monetary values can be challenging and will depends on cross-organisational input (from finance, operations, sales, etc.) to confirm the validity of the best estimate. This exercise can be a time-consuming process if not adequately planned for in advance as part of the need analysis process discussed in Chapter 4.

Where isolation effects are considered, the data collection process can be captured in tiers, first from participants, then reviewed by their managers with the final validation from cross-departmental heads, all of which can be established using a simple questionnaire, interviews or a focus group approach.[13]

An alternative approach to estimating the normalization effects is to apply a more conservative value to the derived ROI computations or by establishing a range of values based on discussions with participant and their managers. Where the participants are at the C-suite level then the CEO and the board can assist in estimating the values of the normalization estimates to be applied to the ROI computation.

Assuming that a ROI of 150 per cent is computed, this can be reduced to, say, 100 per cent to take account of any isolation effects or a range of 100 per cent, 125 per cent and 150 per cent can be quoted. This range can be achieved through sensitivity analysis by considering a number of known normalization effects to determine which factors have the most significant effects on the ROI and this can be achieved through data analytics tools or with the support of an employee with statistical knowledge.

Where possible, data analytics for learning evaluation needs to be integrated into existing project with clear ownership assigned from a member of the c-suite this will ensure that the organisation can maximise the benefits from data-driven decision.[14]

Given the time-lag effects between the incidence of the executive development interventions and when the actual performance effects materialize (discussed in earlier sections of this chapter), it is important to ensure that the normalization factors are considered for the corresponding timeframe to avoid capturing irrelevant factors and thereby dilute the ROI computation.[15]

Finally, with the emergence of AI and machine learning based learning analytics firms such as Zoomi, the processing of data for normalisation will become easier to conduct but the cost may be prohibitive for smaller organisations but more bearable by larger organisations.

Leverage and closing gaps: Once the business impact and ROI has been identified and embedded in an area or division, it is important for the capabilities to be leveraged across other business units or consolidated to drive business model innovations or disruptions in the core and adjacent sectors of the organisation. Where gaps are identified in strategic and value critical business functions and units, appropriate development interventions should be designed to close these gaps to ensure that the organisation does not become exposed to disruptions from competitors. The outputs of this stage can also be fed into the development need analysis process which is detailed in Chapter 4 to help drive improvements in the design of executive development programmes.

For organisations to maximise the value generated from executive development programmes (formal and informal), they must have full commitment from executives and HR functions in terms of allocating adequate resources to collect and analyse data for the various stages of measurement to allow credible evaluation of the return on investment to be computed.

Return on investment and intangibles (ROI/I);

The computation of return on investment on executive development interventions can be derived based on the following:

ROI = (Value generated from development Interventions (normalised/
normalised) - total investment cost)/total delivery cost x 100

A normalised or un-normalised position of the value generated through executive development interventions can be computed based on some single traceable
or dominant interventions undertaken by an executive or cohorts of executives
or by consideration of an amalgamated value based on a number of interrelated or
independent interventions. Where value created is connected to a specific project as in the case of the Cisco SmartGrid example the computation of returns
can be limited to a specific timeline (say, two or three years post implementation). This is owing to the fact that over time these initiatives blend into other
ones and therefore pin-pointing the value created becomes blurred and limit the
capacity to measure the distinctive benefits associated individual initiatives.

For single interventions such as coaching and mentoring, executives can capture the learning touchpoints - such as capability acquisition (or enhancement),
application, anchoring, transferring and embedding including the business
impact - in learning journals or other means and this requires discipline and
support from the organisation including the CEO and board to ensure that this
process is followed and can be tied to performance review processes. A number
of interrelated development interventions targeted at improving a specific intervention can also be tracked cross the learning touchpoints by building a learning
ecosystem (articulating the unique contributions of each interventions within
the cluster of interventions). This approach will provide a structured approach to
help executives to manage the learning journey and business impact assessment.
For example, coaching, reverse mentoring and presentations from thought leaders could all be implemented as development interventions to concurrently addresses gaps in future centricity capabilities of (for example better positioning
for AI, automation and machine learning) an executive cohort. The journaling
process in this instance needs to capture only key takeaway points across each
intervention or only focus on the most impactful interventions (identified based
on participant feedback) and then monitored across the learning touchpoints as
per the approach outlined for the single intervention above. Where the interventions are unrelated to a specific capability but to multiple capabilities, again
some prioritisation needs to take place to limit the data gathering and evaluation
process to focus on the most impactful or significant interventions.

Computation of the total investment cost for informal executive development can be based on hourly rates/pro-rated salaries based on time spent
by executives in engaging in the intervention, application, anchoring and
embedding the capability, including logistics and travelling costs (if the

interventions involves travelling cost to different locations – for job rotation/ multi destination project), IT infrastructure cost (if it involves a technological solution). For example, computation of the cost for development interventions that are based on IT-based systems such simulation, Augmented Reality and Curated Digital content needs to take into account the initial investment outlay and a pro-rated operational cost (estimation of the operational cost which can be attributed to the participants time spend on the system). For example, a simulation programme will consist of initial investment costs (content development, design, acquisition and implementation) and operational costs (support, maintenance, overhead costs, and staff) to provide a robust ROI computation.[16]

Additionally, any costs incurred by the organisation as a result of providing cover for executives whilst they engage in the development intervention may also need to be considered.

To put this into perspective, an executive with a total compensation package of say US$450,000 can translates into the following pre-tax rates (assuming a 40 hour work week with 52 weeks per year and 12 months per year); hourly rate (US$216), daily (US$1,730) and weekly (US$8,653) and hence the compound effect of a number of high-level executives with larger remuneration packages spending time on non-value adding development interventions can possibly results in negative return on investment.

In addition to assessing the return on investment and 'hard' financial benefits which are suitably covered by other existing models, it is important to capture the return of intangibles gained from executive development interventions to provide a holistic picture of how the financial benefits were derived but so that where financial gains take longer to materialise, the intangibles benefits can be an alternative justification for the investment. In addition, these intangibles can have a transformative impact on organisational processes, values and overall management ethos all of which eventually influences the product and service lifecycles and more importantly the capacity to launch disruptive business models. Some of the return in intangibles measures which can be captured include, degree of cultural transformation, enhancement in inter-departmental collaboration, improvement in decision-making effectiveness and employee engagement levels which can be measured through peer-to peer evaluations, 360 degrees feedback, customer and supplier reviews and wider stakeholder feedback systems. This process should also include the review of the volume and value of new ideas, including patents and intellectual property rights and initiatives pending investment that that have been carved out of executive development programmes. Like other tangible measures, intangible measures need to be identified during the need analysis process in consultation with participants and senior executives including potential data collection modes and frequency to minimise any the measurement challenges post-implementation of the development intervention.

Careful planning can also ensure that baseline measures of these intangibles are captured prior to the delivery of the development intervention to offer comparable changes in effects during the post-delivery stage, otherwise there will be nothing to compare against which can either diminish the motivation to measure or base the evaluations on unvalidated perceptions.

In sum this chapter has presented an alternative executive development measurement framework which is more suitable for this cohort and comprising of five key stages: business value impact assessment, capability mastery assessment, capability application and anchoring and transfer assessment, value creation and business impact assessment and ROI/E evaluation. This model will potentially enhance the capacity for organisations to proactively measure the impact of executive development not only to justify further investments in these interventions but also to provide compelling evidence that well-designed and effective development of the executive cohort and the leadership capabilities generated across the organisation drives value creation and long-term organisational survival.

Summary of key issues

Owing to the highly informal nature (stretch projects, network-related learning, coaching) of executive development programmes, measuring the effects of these activities on organisational performance can be challenging and this is compounded further by the time lag effects between when executives engage in development programmes and how long it takes to master and apply new capabilities to drive profitability.

To address some of the limitations of existing measurement models and align them for effective evaluation of executive development programmes, an alternative framework is produced by combining elements of the Kirkpatrick and Philip models with relevant concepts to generate a more compelling one. The resulting executive development evaluation model encapsulating five stages: business value impact assessment, capability mastery assessment, capability application and anchoring and transfer assessment, value creation and business impact assessment and ROI/E evaluation.

The time lag effects can also be counteracted by breaking down the performance measures into intermediary (leading) indicators, short-term indicators and medium-term indicators and putting in place action plans to monitor the leading indicators on a regular basis to ensure successful achievement of the long-term effects of executive development interventions.

The various stages of the executive development evaluation model are juxtaposed against Kirkpatrick's four-level and Philip's five-level models to highlight how it can be applied to drive organisational value and growth.

Evaluating the effects of executive development on organisational impact can be implemented with a number of variations. It can be stand-alone (without isolating the effects of exogenous effects), standalone with exogenous effects normalised, peer review (with participating cohorts) and peer review (with non-participating cohorts).

The executive development evaluation model also provides a means of connecting executive development to clearly defined business drivers which can be translated into objectives / achievable goals and cascaded to multiple levels of an organisation. The focus of application and impact - to provide the proper focus throughout the organisation to drive business value - is also crystallised by this approach.

Measurement of the business impact of executive development interventions is crucial therefore it is important that organisations devote the necessary resources and establish clear guidance on how this will be undertaken. This should take into consideration a number of factors which includes the data capturing process, evaluation options, segmentation and analysis of the data, normalisation and using the data to leveraging and closing gaps in the executive development process.

In addition to assessing the return on investment and 'hard' financial benefits, it is important to capture the return of intangibles gained from executive development interventions to provide a holistic picture of how the financial benefits were derived but so that where financial gains take longer to materialise, the intangibles benefits can be an alternative justification for the investment.

References

1. Piers Lea, LEO Research Results: Year 2 (2017/18) – Emerging trends – Measuring the business impact of learning (Leo Learning 2018) <https://leolearning.com/app/uploads/2018/01/Building_MBIL_strategy_research_results_YR02.pdf (last accessed 2 May 2018).
2. Cisco, 'Cisco Center for Collaborative Leadership' (Cisco 2008) https://www.cisco.com/web/about/ac227/csr2008/our-employees/developing-leaders/executive-development.html (last accessed 20 October 2017).
3. Margaret Alldredge, Cindy Johnson, Jack Stoltzfus and; Al Vicere, 'Leadership development at 3m: new process, new techniques, new growth' (2003) 26 *Human Resource Planning* 45.
4. 3M, '3M Announces New Leadership Development Program: Catalyst Program to Lead the Way in Leadership Development' (3M 29 February 2016) http://news.3m.com/press-release/company-english/3m-announces-new-leadership-development-program (last accessed 20 October 2017).
5. Thunderbird, 'ExxonMobil Advanced Leadership Program' (Thunderbird School of Global Management) https://thunderbird.asu.edu/ExxonMobil-ALP (last accessed 20 October 2017).
6. Duke Corporate Education, 'Verizon: can you hear me now?' http://www.dukece.com/verizon-can-hear-now/ (last accessed 23 October 2017).
7. Magda N. Yrizarry, 'Is there an App for Leadership Development?' (Chief Learning Officer 19 February 2013) http://www.clomedia.com/2013/02/19/is-there-an-app-for-leadership-development/ (last accessed 23 October 2017).

8. Lorri Freifeld, 'Verizon's new number 1 – Verizon rings in 2012 in the top spot on the training top 125' (*Training Magazine* 2012) https://trainingmag.com/content/verizon's-new-number-1 (last accessed 23 October 2017).

9. Caitlin Probst, 'How BP reformulated learning to work like honey bees' (*Degreed* 11 August 2015) http://blog.degreed.com/how-bp-reformulated-learning-to-work-like-honey-bees/ (last accessed 23 October 2017).

10. Robert M. Fulmer and Jared L. Bleak, The Leadership Advantage: How the Best Companies Are Developing Their Talent, to Pave Way for Future Success (AMACOM 2007).

11. Sneha Shah, 'Cisco goes all out to win the Smart Grid Market through Alliance with No.1 Smart Meter Maker Itron and Alta Rock Acquisition' http://www.greenworldinvestor.com/2010/09/05/cisco-goes-all-out-to-win-the-smart-grid-market-through-alliance-with-no-1-smart-meter-maker-itron-and-alta-rock-acquisition (*Green World Investor* 5 September 2010) (last accessed 24 October 2017).

12. Charles Waltner, 'Cisco Creates a New Generation of Collaborative Leaders' (Cisco 7 December 2009) https://newsroom.cisco.com/feature-content?articleId=5263198 (last accessed 25 October 2017).

13. J Phillips and P Phillips, 'Moving from evidence to proof' (2011) 65(8) T+D 34.

14. Academic Conferences and Publishing Limited, '18th European Conference on Knowledge Management (ECKM 2017) 446.

15. Gene Pease, Barbara Beresford, Bonnie Beresford and Lew Walker, Developing Human Capital: Using Analytics to Plan and Optimize Your Learning and Development Investments (Wiley 2014) 155.

16. Hatim Bukhari, Pamela Andreatta, Brian Goldiez and Luis Rabelo, 'A Framework for Determining the Return on Investment of Simulation-Based Training in Health Care' (2017) 54 *The Journal of Health Care Organization, Provision, and Financing* 1.

Index

Information in figures and tables is indicated by page numbers in *italics* and **bold**.